SAFE & CARING SCHOOLS®

SKILLS FOR SCHOOL. SKILLS FOR LIFE.

GRADES 3–5

Katia S. Petersen, Ph.D.

free spirit
PUBLiSHiNG®

Meeting kids'
social & emotional
needs since 1983

Library of Congress Cataloging-in-Publication Data
Petersen, Katia S.
    Safe & caring schools : skills for school. skills for life. / Katia S. Petersen.
        v. cm.
    "Grades 3/5."
            Contents: Skills for school; skills for life—Research foundation—A school-wide commitment—Content overview—SCS monthly themes—Literature base—Lesson plans—Integrated activities—SCS quizzes—Year-round activities—SCS implementation plan—The essential role of leadership—Teaching tips—Parent involvement—Classroom meetings—Year 'round activities—Proven ideas that work—Ambassadors of peace—Caring hearts—Community peace garden—Peace rugs—Feelings mailbox—SCS teacher survey—Year-at-a-glance, grades 3/5—September: me and my safe & caring school—October: discovering our feelings—November: my support system—December: respect yourself and others—January: no bullying—February: teaming up for success—March: getting along with others—April: the power to choose—May: follow your dreams.
        ISBN-13: 978-1-57542-289-3
        ISBN-10: 1-57542-289-1
    1. Classroom management—United States. 2. School environment—United States. 3. Learning, Psychology of. I. Title. II. Title: Safe and caring schools.
        LB3013.P433 2008
        372.1102'4—dc22

                                                                                    2007049588

Edited by Deborah Verdoorn Anderson and John Kober
Visual identity design by Tilka Design
Design by Katrin Loss, Tilka Design, and activity page design by J. Campbell, ArtVille
Illustrations by Brie Spangler

10 9 8 7 6 5 4 3 2 1
Printed in the United States of America

Free Spirit Publishing Inc.
217 Fifth Avenue North, Suite 200
Minneapolis, MN 55401-1299
(612) 338-2068
help4kids@freespirit.com
www.freespirit.com

Dedication

This book is dedicated to the thousands of children in my life who give me inspiration and inner strength to do my part in creating a safe and caring world. It is my hope that these resources help connect children, parents, and educators so they may achieve success wherever life takes them.

Acknowledgments

Safe & Caring Schools (SCS) has been tested where it matters most—in the classrooms. As such, my gratitude goes to all the teachers, specialists, and others who took time to incorporate the content of this guide into their lesson plans and then provide feedback about its efficacy. Efforts to create safe and caring schools are most effective when leadership is committed to applying the program at a schoolwide or district level to create systemic change. My thanks go to Superintendent Dr. Wilfredo T. Laboy and Assistant Superintendent Dr. Mary Lou Bergeron for their foresight regarding the value of social and emotional learning in supporting students personally as well as academically. Dr. Bergeron has been particularly helpful in testing and proving this premise in schools.

Thanks to the staff at Free Spirit Publishing for their dedication to producing great products: To Publisher Judy Galbraith, for her vision and belief in the power of the SCS program. To my editors, John Kober for his ongoing support, guidance, patience and insight during the creation of the products, and Deb Anderson for her extraordinary ability to edit both from her teaching experience and her heart to produce resources that make a difference in the lives of students. And to the production team that pulls all the pieces together to make a book.

Thanks to Jay Campbell at Artville for his professionalism, creativity, and ability to bring the activity pages in this book to life. Also, thanks to my special friends and educators, Kathy Kennedy Budge and Lynn Pauly who listened, offered support, and used their ability to think outside the box to find the best way possible to connect with students.

This book series would not have been completed without the support of my wonderful family. My deepest gratitude goes to my husband, Steve Petersen, for the endless hours he worked by my side, for his ongoing encouragement, his incredible creativity, and for urging me to always reach for excellence. My heartfelt appreciation also goes to my daughter, Alexia, for her patience and support during this project and for reminding me daily about the true meaning of parenting. Warm thanks go to my parents for their unconditional love, for teaching me to believe in myself, and for encouraging me to follow my dreams.

"Safe & Caring Schools provides educators with the roadmap and all the tools necessary to transform classrooms and schools into environments that are not only physically, socially, and emotionally safe, but that engage and nurture our children's resilience, including their capacity and love for learning."

**BONNIE BENARD,
SENIOR PROGRAM ASSOCIATE, WESTED,
OAKLAND, CALIFORNIA**

CONTENTS

FOREWORD

Dr. Katia Petersen has long been a champion for children and has dedicated her career to educating children and adults about the importance of social and emotional development in our youth and ourselves. Her vision, as a practitioner, has been to include life-skills education in the school day. She wants teachers to connect with students in a meaningful way and students to understand the relevance of school and how best to use it as a resource for self-development and well-being. Safe & Caring Schools® is the culmination of more than 25 years of experience working in schools to help educators and others enhance the well-being and emotional literacy skills in children from preschool through high school.

In Safe & Caring Schools, Dr. Petersen has created a comprehensive approach to provide a solid foundation for infusing social and emotional literacy skills—including recognition of emotions, building relationships, conflict resolution, problem-solving, decision-making, and collaboration—into all areas of the program. The activities and resources provided in this book have been field-tested in classrooms across the United States with children from diverse backgrounds. Over the past years, I was fortunate enough to have worked with Dr. Petersen implementing Safe & Caring Schools in the Lawrence Public Schools. During the implementation, we collected a variety of data relative to overall school climate issues. In schools where Safe & Caring Schools was being implemented consistently, the data showed the following:

- an improvement in school climate
- greater parent engagement
- increased academic achievement
- a reduction in referrals for disciplinary infractions

We have continued to use the themes and activities of Safe & Caring Schools as a foundation for the social and emotional development of our students.

As an educator and school psychologist, I understand how children's levels of social and emotional literacy skill development impact their ability to succeed in school. I have seen first-hand how the development of these skills improved the overall academic and social success of our students. As an administrator, I am also acutely aware of the concerns that schools and school districts have relative to time on learning and adding new programs to the school day, especially at a time when there is a heightened focus on academic achievement and a demand for increased instructional time. With this in mind, Safe & Caring Schools was created to be an integrated component of systemic change at the classroom, school, and district levels. It has evolved into an easy-to-use, classroom-based approach that can be infused into all academic content areas with minimal effort on the part of teachers. The skills in the program are universal and can be addressed and reinforced throughout the school day and across grade levels. By infusing social and emotional learning across the curriculum, Safe & Caring Schools provides teachers with the flexibility and creativity they need to ensure students gain the skills they require to become successful students and members of society.

Mary Lou Bergeron, Ph.D.
Assistant Superintendent for
Operations and Support Services
Lawrence Public Schools
Lawrence, Massachusetts

PREFACE

Imagine a world where all children have an opportunity to learn and thrive—a safe place where adults help children become resilient. Imagine the impact safe and caring school communities can make in our challenging world as they encourage peer support, getting along, making ethical choices, problem solving, accountability, and cooperation. With this vision, I created the Safe & Caring Schools (SCS) program to facilitate a blended curriculum of academic and social and emotional learning.

As times have changed, so have the demands put upon educators to meet the needs of every child. But one thing has never changed—the need for all children to feel appreciated, secure, and accepted. Many educators I speak to are concerned, and at times frustrated, about the lack of time to get everything done, the stress of how best to deal with challenging students, and the ever-growing issues of bullying and violence. Research increasingly supports that to reach the whole child, social and emotional learning (SEL) needs to be an integral part of the regular classroom curriculum. But, how much more can schools take on, what kind of support do they need, and how do they deal with the balancing act of mandated standards compliance and reaching children emotionally? SCS is a turnkey, literature-based program that supplies the school staff with a full suite of integrated materials to do this work, not as an add-on, but as part of the daily routine. Years of classroom testing have made Safe & Caring Schools a program that is easy to implement and sustain.

I've spent the past 27 years working in schools with staff and students of all ages, backgrounds, abilities, and talents. Using extensive feedback from thousands of educators, counselors, and parents, Safe & Caring Schools addresses their needs by promoting social and emotional learning in the school, home, and community through the following:

- improving school climate and student behavior
- engaging and motivating students
- increasing academic achievement
- reducing stress
- increasing parent involvement
- enhancing staff teamwork

Time after time in testing this program, the schools that infused SEL into daily activities saw and felt a significant change in the behavior and language of their students. As attitudes and behaviors improved, so did academic performance. As teachers worked together making deliberate plans to embrace the Safe & Caring Schools approach, they created systemic change in a natural way.

My hope is that the content and philosophy of this Safe & Caring Schools resource guide will inspire and help you to enhance your role as a significant adult in your students' lives. I have created a tool that helps you use your wisdom, energy, and desire to reach every child on a personal and emotional level. Every day is a new adventure and an opportunity to create a better world for our children. As you work with SCS materials, I welcome your feedback, success stories, and suggestions for improvements. You can write to me in care of:

Free Spirit Publishing
217 Fifth Avenue North, Suite 200
Minneapolis, MN 55401
or email me at help4kids@freespirit.com

Katia S. Petersen, Ph.D.

PART 1

Skills for School. Skills for Life.

The mission of the Safe & Caring Schools (SCS) program is to create sustainable, positive systemic change by infusing social and emotional learning (SEL) and character education into daily academic instruction from preschool through grade 8. This takes place in partnership with educators, counselors, administrators, parents, and community members to improve academic achievement and school climate.

"When you educate the whole child, you can count on academic growth as well, even if that's not the primary intent." These words from "The Whole Child," a 2007 report from the Association for Supervision and Curriculum Development, reinforce the value of social and emotional learning. SEL is no longer seen as an option to be taught separately from academics; rather, it can be taught and implemented in schools in a number of ways.

SCS supports the idea that reaching the hearts of children is equally as important as reaching their minds. As one teacher explains, "I have learned that if I want my students to succeed academically, I need to teach them how to listen, follow directions, communicate effectively, resolve problems, and make good choices."

Teaching kids life skills needs to become part of the daily routine. Learning to get along with others, accepting responsibility for one's own actions, and making better choices takes practice and needs the guidance and ongoing support from the adults in kids' lives. Consistency and repetition, as well as modeling desirable behaviors, will increase students' ability to internalize and use new skills in real-life situations.

Research Foundation

For several years now, there has been a growing body of scientifically based research supporting the idea that enhanced social and emotional behaviors can have a strong impact on kids' success in school and, ultimately, in life (*Building Academic Success on Social and Emotional Learning: What Does the Research Say?* Edited by Joseph E. Zins, Roger P. Weissberg, Margaret C. Wang, and Herbert J. Walberg. Teachers College Press, Columbia University, 2004). The research substantiates that effective strategies for educational reform involve (1) a central focus on school climate change and (2) infusing SEL into regular academic lesson plans. Giving children a balance of intellectual and emotional instruction leads to more complete psychological development and helps them become better learners. This idea is supported with hard data. For example, The Lucile Packard Foundation for Children's Health and the William T. Grant Foundation funded an analysis of 207 studies of social and emotional learning programs involving 288,000 elementary and secondary students from a cross section of urban, suburban, and rural schools. The results of the analysis are summarized in a 2008 report, "The Benefits of School-Based Social and Emotional Learning Programs" from CASEL (Collaborative for Academic, Social, and Emotional Learning). In evaluating academic outcomes, the study found that in schools where SEL is integrated into the regular programming, students scored 11 percentile points higher on standardized tests compared to students in schools not using an SEL program. Even though incorporating SEL activities required time in the school day, it did not negatively affect students' academic performance; rather, time spent on SEL improved academic performance. This project, conducted by Joseph A. Durlak of Loyola University in Chicago and Roger P. Weissberg at the University of Illinois at Chicago, was the first meta-analysis of research on the impact of SEL programs on students. Their full report is titled *The Effects of Social and Emotional Learning on the Behavior and Academic Performance of School Children.*

SCS incorporates a holistic approach in working with children, combining several research-based strategies into one program in order to nurture the whole child and promote student well-being. SCS defines student well-being as "the development of knowledge, attitudes, skills, and behaviors that maximize students' functioning in environments where they live and work—school, home, and community" (Romano, J. L. *Journal of Educational Research*, 90, 1996). SCS provides you with a comprehensive set of core materials to enhance student well-being in a manner that is easily infused into your daily routine.

SCS materials incorporate a strengths-based approach that fosters resiliency in children to enable them to thrive and become successful in school and in life. Recent research shows that focusing on strengths is one of the key elements in supporting our youth, and schools play a critical role in the development of the strengths or assets in students.

- -

As Bonnie Benard writes in *Resiliency: What We Have Learned* (San Francisco: West Ed, 2004):

A framework, research support, and a rationale for resilience-based prevention and education include the following assumptions:

- *Resilience is a capacity all youth have for healthy development and successful learning.*

- *Certain personal strengths are associated with healthy development and successful learning.*

- *Certain characteristics of families, schools, and communities are associated with the development of personal strengths and, in turn, healthy development and successful learning.*

- *Changing the life trajectories of children and youth from risk to resilience starts with changing the beliefs of the adults in their families, schools, and communities.*

- -

SCS uses a complete and comprehensive plan that makes sense and works.

- It complements and enhances the well-being of children by promoting self-awareness, self-respect, integrity, and compassion to help them become productive citizens of any community.

- It encourages students to take risks and become active learners, regardless of their abilities, language barriers, or cultural differences.

- It leads students to make connections with the world around them by practicing the skills they need to face daily challenges.

- It allows students to realize their potential as positive leaders by providing social and emotional education as part of academic learning.

SCS activities support standards and comply with best practices for SEL infusion at school while providing opportunities for you, the teacher, to use your creativity. When aligned with the key competencies of the Collaborative for Academic, Social, and Emotional Learning (CASEL), the SCS activities clearly address those key SEL competencies: 1) Awareness of self and others, 2) Positive attitudes and values, 3) Responsible decision making, and 4) Social interaction skills.

These SCS materials have been tested with teachers and students of all abilities and backgrounds in public, private, city, and suburban schools. The program has been successful due to the commitment of staff, ongoing support from leadership, and awareness that all student needs—emotional, social, and intellectual—must be met. The schools that had the most success with the program developed strong relationships with their students by infusing SCS principles into the culture of the school, rather than just using occasional add-on SEL or character education units. At these schools, teachers brought the activities to life by modeling desirable behaviors and creating an environment where all students felt safe, accepted, recognized, and celebrated for their individuality every day.

A Schoolwide Commitment

To improve classroom and school climate, the SCS materials can be used by an individual teacher or by an entire school or district. Either approach will work, but a systemic change can be realized only when an entire school makes a commitment to become a safe and caring place. By choosing the schoolwide approach, a school has the benefit of teamwork and support from all staff, plus parents and community members. Through the common language of clear expectations, consistency of messages, modeling of desirable behavior, and the use of vocabulary that will help everyone communicate more effectively, you will be able to create positive systemic change in your school.

To implement a schoolwide SCS program:

- Include social and emotional learning in your mission statement.

- Establish clear expectations for positive behavior.

- Be consistent with expectations and consequences.

- Establish a yearlong plan to reinforce parent involvement.

- Create a support system for all students, staff, and parents.

- Coordinate communication among all staff, including teachers, specialists, administrators, counselors, support staff, substitute teachers, and aides.

- Plan opportunities to recognize and celebrate successes.

Although classroom teachers are the primary implementers of the SCS lessons, administrators, counselors, social workers, health teachers, and other staff can be actively involved in the effort to infuse SEL into all areas of the school. Creating a schoolwide program takes thought and planning, but it's well worth the effort.

"We've seen a significant change in the attitude and the behavior of students. Our suspension rate has dropped, and the infraction rate has dropped significantly. The infraction rate in a sense is the day-to-day business of what's going on in school, and I can see that there's a change. All of these small infractions added up is a big problem, and decreasing them has made a big difference."

PRINCIPAL—TARBOX SCHOOL

PART 2

Content Overview

Students learn best when they see how what they are learning will impact their lives. The more your students can relate to a situation through experiential activities, the more interest they will show in the lesson and the easier it will be for them to apply the skills in real-life situations. This Safe & Caring Schools resource guide includes activities that enable students to have conversations, to learn through inquiry, and to feel empowered to change their own behavior and contribute to the creation of a positive classroom and school culture.

SCS MONTHLY THEMES

The SCS materials provide a sequenced, yet flexible program for social and emotional learning (SEL). Activities are grouped into nine units, one for each month of the typical school year. A theme is designated for each month, so all grade levels using the program have the same monthly theme. This allows each grade level in a schoolwide program to use its specific age-appropriate activities to support the common theme throughout the school. The SCS monthly themes are the following:

– –

SEPTEMBER—Me and My Safe & Caring School

OCTOBER—Discovering Our Feelings

NOVEMBER—My Support System

DECEMBER—Respect Yourself and Others

JANUARY—Bullying

FEBRUARY—Teaming Up for Success

MARCH—Conflict Resolution

APRIL—The Power to Choose

MAY—Follow Your Dreams

– –

Each SCS monthly theme is presented in a brief overview with key objectives to help focus the teaching. The theme is developed with a broad range of literature-based teaching activities, complete with reproducible activity sheets for the students. For easier printing of the activity sheets, they are also available on the CD-ROM included with this book. See pages 12–13 for the "Year-at-a-Glance" chart of all the activities within each monthly theme.

LITERATURE BASE

The SCS activities use children's literature to introduce key concepts, facilitate discussion, and lead into the activities. Using the books promotes active listening, helps increase comprehension, and motivates students to express themselves. The literature connections directly integrate SEL into core academics, making it easy for teachers to "build in" rather than "add on" SCS practices. Check your classroom, school library, or local public library for the books, or acquire some of the titles to start building an SEL library to share with all classrooms. When a suggested book is not available to you, consider another book of your own choosing or simply discuss the key concept of the book as it is described in the lesson plan.

LESSON PLANS

Each activity is presented with simple directions that include the "Learning Objectives," the "Materials Needed," and a four-part teaching plan: ***"READ," "DISCUSS," "DO," "RELATE."*** In "Read," a book related to the activity topic is suggested for shared reading. "Discuss" develops the topic through guided discussion of the book. "Do" provides instructions for using the lesson's activity sheet. "Relate" offers ideas and discussion prompts to connect the topic to the students' daily lives, and these ideas can be good writing prompts for journal entries.

The activities are designed to be used as starting points to introduce the key concepts of a safe and caring school. With open conversation, kids will gain a better understanding of the concepts and a sense of ownership of their own growth. See pages 12–13 for the "Year-at-a-Glance" chart of all the activities within each monthly theme.

INTEGRATED ACTIVITIES

In addition to the more than 100 lesson plans, ideas for integrating each monthly theme across curricular areas—language arts, literature, art, music, and math—are provided to follow up and expand on topics.

ASSESSMENT

Best practices include ongoing assessment for program mastery. The final activity sheet for each month is a short quiz to assess the students' grasp of the concepts related to the monthly theme. Three types of questions and a writing activity are included. You may choose to use a quiz as a pre- and post-test to demonstrate where students started and how far they have grown by unit's end.

YEAR-ROUND ACTIVITIES

To support the success of a schoolwide effort, a set of activities that can be implemented at the start of the school year and used throughout the year is included (pages 7–9). These activities provide the school with a common vision and language that will maximize the benefits of the SCS program.

SCS Implementation Plan

The SCS activities have been successfully used in homerooms, regular classroom settings, during advisory time, and as part of before- and after-school childcare and various youth or club programs.

Classroom teachers are commonly the primary implementers of the SCS lessons. Materials can be used independently in each classroom, but for systemic change, schools should consider a building-wide program. When all school staff—including teachers, administrators, counselors, social workers, media specialist, aides, coaches, support staff, and childcare providers—are involved in supporting the program, the students benefit from consistency of message and modeling of positive behavior. Schoolwide implementation creates an environment where students know what is expected of them, no matter where they are or what activities they are involved in throughout the day. To support the success of schoolwide implementation, it is essential for all staff to understand the philosophy of the SCS program—its goals, objectives, and action plan—and to be committed to working as a team to create a safe and caring school.

Counselors and social workers can use the program in small, student support groups during the school day, as part of after-school activities, or for parent presentations. In one-on-one situations, the activities can be used to practice specific skills, such as being assertive, using "I-messages," or diffusing negative situations. We have observed counselors and social workers playing a leadership role in promoting a comprehensive approach in the way SCS is used by all staff.

Media specialists and librarians have supported the schoolwide monthly theme by selecting appropriate reading and audiovisual materials for classes. Children can read the books alone, or the media specialist can have read-aloud sessions and discuss how the book's characters feel, express their emotions, deal with conflict, and resolve problems.

An SCS library corner can be set up so staff and students know which books to read to support the theme of each month. Social studies, writing, and art teachers can provide support with SCS theme-based projects.

The Essential Role of Leadership

Children look to the adults around them for guidance, support, and safety. As the leaders of your school and classroom communities, you set the tone for the school year. To create a safe and caring school and achieve long-term positive change, the following strategies are recommended:

In a schoolwide program:

- **Mission.** Identify creating a safe and caring school as a schoolwide goal.

- **Core Team.** Assign a group to oversee the SCS program to keep implementation on track. The core team may be teachers from each grade level or a combination of teachers, administrators, support staff, specialists, and parents.

- **Action Plan.** Create and communicate an implementation plan to all staff, parents, and the community. Keep the lines of communication open so everyone has a voice.

- **Professional Development.** Use training and department planning to enhance the instructional process and effectively use new materials. Plan to train new teachers each year in the SCS program through in-service and teacher mentoring. Provide ongoing support, positive feedback, and a chance to celebrate progress.

- **Comprehensive Approach.** Fully integrate SEL into the daily curriculum and the daily life of students and teachers.

In the classroom:

- **Clear Expectations.** Have students help you create the classroom rules. Their active involvement will lead to positive engagement.
- **Follow Through.** Let students know you are committed to making sure everyone feels safe and has the right to learn and enjoy being in your classroom. Following through shows them you mean what you say.
- **Connect with Each Child.** Get to know your students at the beginning of the year. This will help you build strong, trusting relationships. As you invest in them, they will invest in you.
- **No Tolerance.** Explain to students the meaning of no tolerance for violence, harassment, and negative behavior. Conflicts are a normal part of life, but bullying and harassing others in your safe and caring school are not.

Teaching Tips

There are no simple answers or quick fixes that will create the kind of school community you and your students will want to be a part of every day. But there are a number of things you can do to engage kids in the process of learning to get along with others and accepting responsibility for their own actions. Here are a few suggestions.

BEST PRACTICES

Because the SCS materials are group-graded, plan to meet regularly (at least monthly) with all the teachers using the same book to determine which activities everyone will use. You may want to use some activities at all grade levels to support the schoolwide program, while reserving others for a specific grade level. Keep in mind that some repetition of activities is a good thing because it aids in learning and reinforcing key concepts.

You can take several steps to help make the SCS program successful:

- Become familiar with the material. Review this resource guide in its entirety prior to using it.
- Be flexible. Use your creativity and knowledge to adapt the activities to meet the needs of your students.
- Be positive. Motivate and inspire your students.

- Diversify your teaching style. This SCS resource guide provides you with a diverse range of activities that enable you to work with multiple learning styles.
- Develop a cohesive group of students. Use small groups and pairs of students to complete many of the activities. Vary the way groups are formed—try counting off; odd and even numbers; using colors of clothes, shoes, eyes, or hair; alphabetical order; height; letting students choose (be sensitive to problems of exclusion), or other creative ways.

When lessons have personal meaning to students, they are more likely to change their behavior because they want to, rather than because they are told to do so. To motivate your students and make the lessons personal, keep these best practices in mind:

- Help children understand the new skills and why they matter to them.
- Demonstrate what the new skill looks like, sounds like, and feels like.
- Create opportunities for children to practice their new skills.
- Consider the use of journal writing to help kids personalize their new skills.
- Use teachable moments to correct and redirect children.
- Celebrate the students who adopt desirable behaviors in school.
- Model the new social and emotional skills as often as possible.
- Infuse SEL into academic subject areas.

PARENT INVOLVEMENT

Involve parents and guardians in the SCS process. Once you establish your classroom and school expectations, send a copy of them to the parents and guardians of all students. Enclose a short letter explaining how the SCS program works in your classroom and school. Explain that you are actively teaching children social and emotional skills along with academics, and include the advantages of doing so. Ask for their support to help children practice the same expectations and skills at home for reinforcement and consistency. Keep the parents actively involved—send home tips, ideas, success stories, and pictures from events at your safe and caring school. Encourage parents to visit your classroom to help with specific activities.

CLASSROOM MEETINGS

Misunderstandings at school, teasing, bullying, or use of inappropriate language can turn into big problems that take time away from your teaching. Be proactive by using classroom meetings (sometimes called "circle time") to address these issues. By doing so, you create a forum where students can share their feelings, as well as review, process, and discuss ways to positively resolve conflicts.

Classroom meetings give you the opportunity to get to know your students better and allow you to build stronger relationships. Students have the opportunity to practice listening, taking turns, sharing feelings, showing empathy for others, problem solving, and making decisions. Explain to your students the purpose of these meetings and establish clear expectations so students feel safe to participate. You may want to start with these instructions:

- Use active listening.
- Wait for your turn to speak.
- Don't use put-downs.
- Respect everyone's feelings and ideas.
- It's okay to disagree.
- You have the right to pass.

Morning meetings give you a sense of how your students feel, which helps you set the tone for the day. Ask your students to share something that is happening in their lives. This is also a good time to review your expectations and give students a quick preview of the day's activities.

Midday meetings work well for students who return from lunch, recess, or special events with complaints or hurt feelings. When these feelings are not addressed, they can contribute to the students' inability to focus on the learning activities.

End-of-the-day meetings cover unfinished business, review the day, celebrate accomplishments, and remind students that you look forward to seeing them the next day. Students who leave school feeling isolated, hurt, threatened, or bullied on a regular basis often choose to skip school. Providing a safe environment for sharing feelings and resolving conflicts in a timely fashion will help the students feel secure and ready to come back the next day. It takes only one caring adult to make a difference in a child's life.

Emergency meetings give you the time you need to confront issues as they happen so you can go back to teaching and students can complete their day without interference. The key is to be proactive and redirect your students before negative behaviors get out of control.

When students share too much personal information during meetings, explain the difference between private and public information. Take time to explain confidentiality and the importance of respecting each other's privacy. If a child refers to anything at home that sounds like an abusive situation, don't discuss it in class but bring it to the attention of the school administrator.

Year-Round Activities

You will want to implement some or all of these ideas and yearlong activities to build a positive school climate and create a safe and caring community for staff, students, and parents. Implementing these ideas at the start of the year and continuing to use them throughout the school year will support the common SCS vision, language, and expectations.

TEN IDEAS THAT WORK

1. Use grade level or department meetings to review expectations, rules, and support resources, and to discuss other topics related to SCS implementation.

2. Provide a monthly Ambassadors of Peace celebration (see below).

3. Decorate hallways and bulletin boards to promote your safe and caring school. Each month have a designated classroom display some of their completed activities.

4. Use morning announcements to communicate monthly themes and the monthly vocabulary (see first activity of each month).

5. In a parent newsletter, include the monthly theme with tips and ideas for home and family use.

6. Display the SCS Posters (available separately) in classrooms and throughout the school in common areas.

7. Have books related to the SCS themes featured in the library or classrooms.

8. Involve the student council or other student groups in promoting the messages of being a safe and caring school.

9. Use peer teaching by having older students teach monthly activities to younger students through reading, writing, drama, or art.

10. Include school nurses, health teachers, and other school resource people in promoting safe and healthy choices.

AMBASSADORS OF PEACE

The "Ambassadors of Peace" activity (page 20) recognizes students for making good choices, resolving conflicts in peaceful ways, and practicing their positive character skills. Use the "Ambassadors of Peace" poster to remind students of the skills they need to work on to support a safe and caring school.

To conclude each month's SCS activities, nominate one or two students per classroom as ambassadors of peace for practicing their skills of peacemaking, such as making good choices, being respectful, or helping others. Have classroom teachers, counselors, or students nominate students by describing their specific peacemaking attributes. Create an Ambassadors of Peace nomination form using this model.

Safe & Caring Schools
AMBASSADOR OF PEACE NOMINATION

Date_____

I nominate _____

as an Ambassador of Peace because_____

_____

_____ .

Signed_____

Plan an Ambassadors of Peace celebration, which might be a classroom party, a schoolwide or department assembly, or a grade-level breakfast. Invite each nominee's family to attend the celebration. Follow up with phone calls to encourage parents, other family members, or friends to attend.

During the celebration, present the children with Ambassadors of Peace certificates, buttons, or pendants. Give parents the nomination forms so they know why their children were chosen as Ambassadors of Peace. (For example, Marina is an excellent listener, a great friend, and is helpful and respectful to everyone.)

You may choose to acknowledge the Ambassadors of Peace on the same day as a "Student of the Month" celebration. This coordinates the two programs into an existing initiative, which may be easier than finding time for two things in a busy school calendar.

CARING HEARTS

Catching kids doing the right thing and highlighting the positive behavior you see will motivate students to change negative behavior. Give children paper hearts each time they are caught using positive character skills, such as showing kindness, sharing, working together, or making good choices.

One option is to hand out the hearts every day and then collect them at the end of the week. Create a "Caring Hearts Tree" on a wall or door. Add the hearts to it each week, so children can see how often they use their new skills. The goal is to create an environment where all children have an opportunity to be recognized and to celebrate positive change. Encourage parent volunteers to help you cut out as many hearts as possible so they are available to you at all times.

Remember that each day is a new beginning and another chance to succeed at learning something new. Hearts are not to be taken away if a student makes a bad choice. Redirecting behavior and giving students a reminder of what is needed to earn a heart will teach responsibility for one's actions.

COMMUNITY PEACE GARDEN

To practice teamwork skills, listening to and following directions, and taking responsibility, involve the students, parents, and community in creating a garden. The peace garden can be a place where individuals or groups go when they need a quiet moment or need to resolve an issue before it becomes a big conflict. This is a good project in which to involve parents, community volunteers, gardeners, garden shops, carpenters, and home supply stores for donated time, expertise, and materials.

Choose a spot—outside, inside, or both—for your garden. (If inside, use potted plants and indoor benches or chairs in the garden.) With some expert help, build wooden benches to place in the garden. Prepare the soil for planting. When it is ready, plant flowers, bulbs, trees, and shrubs. Decorate the area with rocks, and have the children paint words of peace on the rocks. (You could use words and phrases from the SCS themes.) Add posts in the garden that can be used to display the children's artwork during the year. As you work together on the garden, reinforce lessons of teamwork, cooperation, responsibility, caring, and nurturing. Don't forget to have a community celebration once your garden is complete. Work together to provide ongoing care for the garden.

PEACE RUGS

Children can use carpet squares, which you can call "Peace Rugs," as the setting to resolve conflicts in peaceful ways. After you model the steps of resolving a conflict without hurting the other person physically or emotionally (pages 136–142), give students opportunities to practice using role-play situations. When real conflicts arise, students will be able to use this process on their own without disrupting the class. It might take longer for some students than others to understand that they can resolve conflicts together, but it is worth the effort to get to that point. No matter how big or small the conflicts that students face daily, the skills of problem solving and decision making are ones they will use for a lifetime.

The process starts with kids sitting on their peace rugs face-to-face. Have them take turns sharing responses to these questions: What's the problem? How do I feel about it? What choices do I have? What can I do to make things better? When students are done talking and reach an agreement on what to do, have them shake hands or give a high five. Make sure to follow up with them later to see if the plan is working.

FEELINGS MAILBOX

Create a classroom mailbox and label it "Feelings Mailbox." With all you try to accomplish during the day, it is not always possible to recognize the emotions and address the concerns of your students in a timely manner. The feelings mailbox is a safe place where students can leave confidential messages for you when they need adult support. Go through the box daily so you can decide the urgency and the type of support a student needs.

"One way I'm able to integrate the Safe & Caring Schools is through read-alouds and reflection papers that connect the story we read to a child's own life. It's really become the central part of my classroom. And I feel as though the children as a result have developed better bonds between each other."

TEACHER—SOUTH LAWRENCE
EAST SCHOOL

TEACHER SURVEY—PART 1
SCHOOL/CLASSROOM CLIMATE

Using the 1 to 5 scale, circle the response that best describes your actions and proficiency at this time.
1 = Consistently   2 = Often   3 = Occasionally   4 = Infrequently   5 = Never

1. I set clear expectations in my classroom.	1	2	3	4	5
2. I enforce classroom and schoolwide expectations.	1	2	3	4	5
3. I teach students about being accountable for their own actions.	1	2	3	4	5
4. I recognize my students for using their social and emotional skills by choosing them as Ambassadors of Peace.	1	2	3	4	5
5. I develop a sense of community in my classroom.	1	2	3	4	5
6. I use circle time/classroom meetings to review new ideas and to practice social and emotional literacy.	1	2	3	4	5
7. I use cooperative groups to reinforce teamwork and peer teaching.	1	2	3	4	5
8. I model and use teachable moments to reinforce social and emotional learning in the lessons I teach.	1	2	3	4	5
9. I teach social and emotional literacy by infusing activities from the Safe and Caring Schools resource guide.	1	2	3	4	5
10. I teach students strategies to help them deal with bullying behavior.	1	2	3	4	5
11. I teach students conflict resolution and problem-solving strategies.	1	2	3	4	5
12. I meet with other staff to discuss and plan schoolwide activities to reinforce social and emotional learning.	1	2	3	4	5
13. I seek support from my colleagues when problems arise in my classroom so I can solve them more effectively.	1	2	3	4	5
14. I assess the effectiveness of my efforts to include social and emotional learning in my daily teaching practice.	1	2	3	4	5
15. I connect with parents to be partners in teaching and supporting social and emotional learning at home as in school.	1	2	3	4	5

TEACHER SURVEY—PART 2
SKILLS AND KNOWLEDGE

Using the 1 to 5 scale, circle the response that best describes your actions and proficiency at this time.
1 = Consistently   2 = Often   3 = Occasionally   4 = Infrequently   5 = Never

1. My students feel safe at school.	1	2	3	4	5
2. My students understand the school and classroom expectations.	1	2	3	4	5
3. My students follow the school and classroom expectations.	1	2	3	4	5
4. My students know how to ask for help.	1	2	3	4	5
5. My students use conflict-resolution skills to deal with problems.	1	2	3	4	5
6. My students identify and express their emotions appropriately.	1	2	3	4	5
7. My students use good manners.	1	2	3	4	5
8. My students show respect toward adults and students.	1	2	3	4	5
9. My students show empathy toward others.	1	2	3	4	5
10. My students appropriately deal with bullying behavior at school.	1	2	3	4	5
11. My students practice active listening.	1	2	3	4	5
12. My students demonstrate the ability to make good choices.	1	2	3	4	5
13. My students recognize their gifts and talents.	1	2	3	4	5
14. My students know how to set goals.	1	2	3	4	5
15. My students have positive dreams for the future.	1	2	3	4	5

Year-at-a-Glance, Grades 3–5

Use this chart as a planning tool to review the SCS concepts and topics for the school year. You will see that the activities support the monthly theme and there is a logical progression to the order of the themes. Of course, it is possible to adjust the order of the themes to better fit with your curriculum or with other schoolwide events. Be creative with your planning and teaching.

Along with your teaching colleagues, select the activities you will use in your classroom each month. For example, you may decide that each 3rd grade teacher will devote 30 minutes to the

same activity on the same day, or within the same week. Since this is a group-graded resource guide, be sure you are involving all the appropriate teachers in the planning.

Also, you can use this chart to help you plan ahead to gather the books you want to use as the literature base for each lesson. The suggested book for each activity is listed opposite the activity name. See the activity directions for additional literature suggestions.

THEME	ACTIVITY TITLE—LITERATURE CONNECTION	
September Me and My Safe & Caring School	SCS Vocabulary Activities Safe & Caring Promise—*The Promise Quilt* Safe & Caring Rules—*Miss Nelson Is Missing* Golden Rule—*Miss Yonkers Goes Bonkers* My Safe & Caring School—*The Brand New Kid* Our Classroom Community—*The Streets Are Free*	All About Us—*Amazing Grace* You and Me—*What I Like About Me* My Family—*Celebrating Families* My Positive Traits—*The Name Jar* Ambassadors of Peace—*Peace Begins with You* Quiz
October Discovering Our Feelings	SCS Vocabulary Activities Feelings Smoothie—*A to Z: Do You Ever Feel Like Me?* How Do You Feel?—*The Boys' & Girls' Book of Dealing with Feelings* What Can I Do When I Get Angry?—*Dealing with Anger* The Anger Meter—*Is It Right to Fight?* Stop, Think, Choose—*Feelings*	I-Messages—*Learning About Assertiveness from the Life of Oprah Winfrey* Feelings and Actions—*How to Take the Grrrr Out of Anger* Patience Please—*I Can't Wait* Guess That Feeling—*Angel Child, Dragon Child* What Do You Tell Yourself?—*Shrinking Violet* Quiz
November My Support System	SCS Vocabulary Activities People I Can Count On—*The Rag Coat* Amazing Changes—*Always and Forever* What Is a Friend?—*How to Be a Friend* Recipe for a Friend—*How Kids Make Friends: Secrets for Making Lots of Friends, No Matter How Shy You Are* Give and Take—*How to Lose All Your Friends*	Gift from the Heart—*The Wednesday Surprise* Stressing the Positive—*Don't Pop Your Cork on Mondays!* They Made Me Do It—*It's Not My Fault!* Caring About Compassion—*Thank You, Mr. Falker* Getting Help and Helping Others—*Chicken Sunday* Quiz
December Respect Yourself and Others	SCS Vocabulary Activities Compliment Calendar—*Princess Penelope's Parrot* Time for Respect—*Crow Boy* A Better Way to Say It—*Manners* Lining Up Good Manners—*Mrs. Peloki's Substitute* My Story of Acceptance—*Grandmama's Pride*	I'm Not to Blame—*Arthur and the True Francine* My Apologies—*Sorry!* Let's Be Honest—*The Empty Pot* Equality and Stereotypes—*Trading Places with Tank Talbott* Nobody Left Out—*A Day's Work* Quiz

Month / Theme	Activities
January Bullying	SCS Vocabulary Activities Too Quick to Judge—*Enemy Pie* The Problem with Bullying—*My Secret Bully* Mean Words Hurt—*But Names Will Never Hurt Me* A Kid's View on Bullies—*Stop Picking on Me* Helping Our Friends Stop Bullying—*Nobody Knew What to Do* The Other Person's Shoes—*Say Something* Just Kidding—*Just Kidding* Stop the Tease Monster Game—*The Meanest Thing to Say* It's Okay to Tell Sometimes—*Telling Isn't Tattling* Courageous and Safe—*The Ant Bully* Quiz
February Teaming Up for Success	SCS Vocabulary Activities Responsibility Rocks!—*Dealing with Choices* Portrait of a Leader—*Speak Up and Get Along!* Cooperation and Me—*Pitch In! Kids Talk About Cooperation* Teamwork Means Everybody!—*Teamwork* Test Your Teamwork—*City Green* Making Decisions—*Christina Katerina and the Time She Quit the Family* Sharing in Teams—*We Are a Team* A Great Team!—*The Giant Turnip* All Together Now—*Oliver Onion: The Onion Who Learns to Accept and Be Himself* Leaders and Followers—*The Berenstain Bears and the Trouble with Friends* Quiz
March Conflict Resolution	SCS Vocabulary Activities Totally Listening—*The Surprise Party* Listen Up!—*My Momma Likes to Say* Get the Whole Story—*My Teacher Likes to Say* Picture This—*Brave as a Mountain Lion* Cool Response—*I Hate Everyone* All About Conflict—*The Paper Bag Princess* Who's In Charge of Me?—*Don't Rant and Rave on Wednesdays!* Special Report—*Potatoes, Potatoes* Stop, Think, Choose Confidence Cruise—*Wilma Unlimited: How Wilma Rudolph Became the World's Fastest Woman* Change of Attitude—*Chocolatina* Quiz
April The Power to Choose	SCS Vocabulary Activities I Have the Power to Choose—*Easing the Teasing* Making Positive Choices—*Elbert's Bad Word* Targeting Good Choices—*The Handbook for Helping Kids with Anxiety and Stress* Choose Wisely—*Pedrito's Day* Choice Week—*Too Many Tamales* Choices & Consequences Cards—*More If You Had to Choose, What Would You Do?* Fair and Unfair—*Bean Thirteen* Helping Make School Safe & Caring—*Arthur's Computer Disaster* Good Friends Help Make Good Choices—*More If You Had to Choose, What Would You Do?* Save the Earth!—*Earth Day—Hooray!* Quiz
May Follow Your Dreams	SCS Vocabulary Activities Heroes—*The Black Snowman* Lots to Celebrate—*Dancing in the Wings* Job Charades—*When I Grow Up* Who Do You Call?—*Boy, Can He Dance!* Dream Steps—*Ziggy's Blue Ribbon Day* When I Grow Up, My Dream Is to Be—*Someday* Perseverance—*America's Champion Swimmer: Gertrude Ederle* Safe, Caring, & Inspired—*Dare to Dream! 25 Extraordinary Lives* Safe & Caring You—*We Were There, Too! Young People in U.S. History* Mobilize Your Dreams—*Zora Hurston and the Chinaberry Tree* Safe & Caring End-of-Year Celebration—*Leonardo, Beautiful Dreamer* Quiz

SEPTEMBER
Me and My Safe & Caring School

- **Setting Expectations**
- **Classroom Community**
- **Social Awareness**

- **Self-Awareness and Acceptance**
- **Belonging**

Children grow strong when they receive unconditional love, ongoing support, and positive recognition. Before we can begin to teach them about getting along, solving problems peacefully, making good choices, and making friends, we need to help them understand the amazing journey of self-discovery they can have at school. To learn to care for others, children first have to learn to care for themselves.

MONTHLY OBJECTIVES
Students will:

- learn about and participate in setting up a safe and caring classroom community
- understand they are unique and learn to recognize, empathize with, and respect the individuality and diversity of others
- experience the importance of inclusion, belonging, and celebrating their families

TEACHING TIPS

- Setting clear expectations and teaching students how to interact with one another are the first steps to learning how to get along.
- It is essential to define the desirable and expected behavior of your students.
- Students thrive when they know that who they are, what they say, and what they do matters to their teacher. Recognize them for their efforts to do well academically and socially.

In addition to the specific lesson plans for this month, you can use these optional ideas to integrate and extend the Safe & Caring themes into daily routines and across the curricular areas.

LANGUAGE ARTS

- Determine appropriate classroom rules with your students. Discuss the benefits of having and following rules.

- Brainstorm what it means to be unique. Encourage students to write stories that describe how they are unique individuals. Use the stories to create a classroom book on individuality. During the first month of the school year, have students read their stories to the group during class meeting time.

LITERATURE

- Ask students to read a story about inclusion and share personal experiences of how it feels to be included and excluded from a group.

- Have students do a library search for a book on individuality, uniqueness, or acceptance (for example, *I Like Being Me* by Judy Lalli). Have students read alone or with a partner. Then, have a "Book Review Day" and ask students to take turns being book critics, sharing what they liked or disliked about the book they read.

ART

- Create collages showing the importance of belonging. Choose pictures or other items that represent people working, playing, or helping one another to create a safe community.

- Begin a quilt project to celebrate the ethnic and cultural diversity within your classroom. Add squares to the quilt as you study new countries and cultures. Consider the following:
  - *The Sunflower Quilting Bee at Arles* by Faith Ringgold depicts African-American women making a quilt with Vincent van Gogh.
  - *Tar Beach* by Faith Ringgold will inspire students to use pictures to tell their stories about their families and the things they do together.
  - *Dancing at the Louvre: Faith Ringgold's French Collection and Other Story Quilts* can be used as inspiration for creating story quilts of your own.
  - Compare Hmong storycloths (pa'ndau) to story quilts. How are they alike and different?

- Create "Welcome to Our Safe and Caring School" greeting cards for new students.

MUSIC

- Play music that covers the topics of celebration, community, respect, and individuality. Good examples include the following:
  - *Ready to Rock Kids, Volumes 1 & 2* (Activity Books and Music CDs) by Dr. Mac & Friends
  - "You've Got a Friend in Me" (duet version), Randy Newman and Lyle Lovett, *Toy Story* soundtrack, Walt Disney Records

- Have students listen to songs that have words related to the monthly theme. Then, in small groups and using known melodies, have students write their own songs based on the theme.

MATH

- As a follow up to the "You and Me" activity (page 19), create a Venn diagram showing the similarities and differences between the partners.

- Use information from the "My Family" activity (page 19) to create graphs that show how many people are in students' families, how many males versus females, how many siblings, how many pets, and the cultural heritage.

- Have students create a color-by-number activity that uses math problems to determine how to color quilt-square designs.

- Use the activities from either of these books by Cindi Mitchell to practice math skills and discover the many variations of shapes and colors that can be used to create quilts: *Quilt Math* or *Math Skills Made Fun/Quilt Math*.

Safe & Caring Vocabulary and Word Find

LEARNING OBJECTIVES

Students will:

- be introduced to vocabulary that supports learning how they should behave in a safe and caring classroom
- internalize the vocabulary as they use it throughout the month and year in real-life situations

MATERIALS NEEDED

"Safe & Caring Vocabulary" (page 21) and "Safe & Caring Word Find" (page 22) activity sheets, dictionaries, pencils

LESSON PLAN

Use the vocabulary activities to introduce the concepts and common language associated with this month's theme. Throughout the month, use the words in writing, spelling, storytelling, and dealing with conflict situations.

For "Safe & Caring Schools Vocabulary," explain how to use the secret code to decipher the message. (In our _safe_ and _caring school_, our _classroom community_ has _rules_ to help us _get along_. The most _important_ rule is to treat _others_ the way we want to be treated, with _respect_. We all have ways that we are _similar_ and _different_. To make our school a _fun_ place to _learn_, we _pledge_ to help everyone feel like they _belong_.)

For "Safe & Caring Word Find," discuss what the words mean after completing the page. You may want students to work in pairs to help each other.

Safe & Caring Promise

LEARNING OBJECTIVES

Students will:

- learn the meaning of a promise or pledge
- make a commitment to work together to create a safe and caring school

MATERIALS NEEDED

The book _The Promise Quilt_ by Candice F. Ransom, a copy of "Safe & Caring Promise" miniposter (page 23), and pens, pencils, or markers

LESSON PLAN

READ   _The Promise Quilt._ Addie's father promises her that she will go to school. When he does not return from the war, she feels that he has broken his promise, and fears that she will never learn to read and write. But with her mother's hard work, they sew and sell a quilt that helps buy school supplies so Addie can go to school.

DISCUSS   What did Addie's father promise her before he left for the war? How did Addie feel when her father did not return? What solution did her mother find to help her go to school? If you could add to the end of the story, what would you write about?

DO   Show the "Safe & Caring Promise" miniposter. Read the promise and discuss the meaning of the words. Place the poster on a table and have the children sign it, signifying their personal commitment to do their part in helping make their school a safe place for everyone. Display the poster in a prominent place in the room.

RELATE   the activity to real life by talking about pledges and promises. Ask: With what pledges are you familiar? Why do people break promises? Do you always keep your promises? How do you feel when promises are broken? Why is keeping a promise important? Explain that they can read the Safe & Caring Promise throughout the year as a reminder of their commitment to help each other get along.

Safe & Caring Rules

LEARNING OBJECTIVES

Students will:

- understand the importance of rules and the consequences of not following them
- learn what behaviors are expected of them on school grounds

MATERIALS NEEDED

The book *Miss Yonkers Goes Bonkers* by Mike Thaler, a copy of "Safe & Caring Rules" miniposter (page 24)

LESSON PLAN

READ *Miss Yonkers Goes Bonkers*. A class knows they will not have an ordinary day when they experience the antics of their teacher who, with spitballs and paper airplanes, outdoes the worst of her students' bad behavior.

DISCUSS Help the students define *rule*. What would happen if students and grown-ups stopped following rules? Why do we need rules? (*Rules keep us safe; they help us get along; they give us ideas of what is expected of us so we don't get in trouble.*) What kind of classroom would you like to be in all year? (*fun, peaceful, safe, respectful, kind*) What might happen if the rules are broken? What are consequences? What can we do as a group to make sure we follow our classroom rules?

DO Show the "Safe & Caring Rules" miniposter. Using role plays, illustrate different situations that show how to follow the rules. (For example, to help students learn the rule about listening, model what the rule sounds like, feels like, and looks like.) Have students come up with additional role plays.

RELATE the miniposter to classroom life by reviewing the rules during teachable moments. Nothing is more powerful than a lesson from a real-life experience. Remember to set and reinforce clear expectations daily. Help students learn how to interact with others in positive ways by modeling desirable behaviors. Recognize kids when they follow the rules. Display the poster in your room.

Golden Rule

LEARNING OBJECTIVES

Students will:

- define *respect* and equate it with the meaning of the golden rule
- use math, drawing, and story writing to explore the application of the golden rule in their lives

MATERIALS NEEDED

The book *Miss Nelson Is Missing* by Harry Allard, copies of "Golden Rule" miniposter (page 25) and "The Golden Rule" activity sheet (page 26), and pencils, pens, or markers

LESSON PLAN

READ *Miss Nelson Is Missing*. The kids in room 207 take advantage of their teacher's good nature until she disappears and they are challenged by her substitute, Viola Swamp.

> An optional story for more in-depth discussion is *Rules* by Cynthia Lord. Set in coastal Maine, this sensitive story is about being and feeling different. This is a great discussion starter about understanding and finding acceptance.

DISCUSS Why did Miss Nelson disappear? What did the children learn about following rules?

DO a group reading of the "Golden Rule" miniposter after distributing a copy to everyone. Discuss the rule in light of the story you read. Note that this is the most important rule for getting along. Brainstorm and make a list of ways students can practice using the golden rule.

Distribute "The Golden Rule" activity sheet. After "doing the math," have students define the word *respect* and describe three ways they can choose to show respect to others. Ask students to write a personal story about a time they learned about respect.

RELATE the activity to students' lives by having volunteers share their stories and drawings. Collect the activity sheets and create an "Our Golden Rule" classroom book.

My Safe & Caring School

LEARNING OBJECTIVES

Students will:

- learn how to make their school a safe and caring place by identifying what a safe and caring school looks like, sounds like, and feels like
- learn the difference between inclusion and exclusion, and steps they can take to include others

MATERIALS NEEDED

The book *The Brand New Kid* by Katie Couric, copies of "My Safe & Caring School" (page 27), and pencils, pens, or markers

LESSON PLAN

READ *The Brand New Kid*. Lazlo is a new kid in class, and he is teased and excluded starting day one. Eventually, Ellie, a girl from his class, begins to wonder what it must be like to be the new kid, and she decides to get to know Lazlo, even at the risk of facing her friends' ridicule.

DISCUSS How did Lazlo feel being the new kid in class? How did the other students treat him? What did Ellie do to help him feel better? How did her friends respond to her after she chose to help Lazlo?

DO the "My Safe & Caring School" activity sheet by having partners work together. For ideas on how to select partners, see "Teaching Tips" on page 6. Have student pairs take turns sharing their ideas about what makes a school a safe and caring place. Refer back to the set of rules students helped you create to support working together to make their school a safe place. Discuss what it means to have a sense of ownership and pride in their school.

RELATE the lesson to daily life in the classroom by helping students develop a better understanding of acceptance and treating others with respect regardless of differences and abilities. Ask: What can we do to help students feel part of our group or school community? How would you feel if you were teased or excluded by other students? Why is it important to get to know each other? How does it feel to make new friends and become a member of a school community?

Our Classroom Community

LEARNING OBJECTIVES

Students will:

- explore how a school classroom is like a community
- review the rules and expectations they need in order to have a safe classroom community

MATERIALS NEEDED

The book *The Streets Are Free* by Kurusa, copies of "Our Classroom Community" activity sheet (page 28), dictionaries, and pens, pencils, or markers

LESSON PLAN

READ *The Streets Are Free*, a creative story about a group of children who decide to work together to help create a more safe and fun community.

DISCUSS What is the meaning of the word *community*? What does it mean to belong in a safe community, such as home or school? Brainstorm ways students can make sure everyone feels safe.

DO the "Our Classroom Community" activity sheet, having students work in pairs to complete it.

RELATE the activity to daily life by having the paired students share their ideas about ways for everyone to work together to make their classroom a safe and caring community.

All About Us

LEARNING OBJECTIVES

Students will:

- have an opportunity to learn more about their classmates
- recognize how each person is unique and learn to appreciate the individuality of others

MATERIALS NEEDED

The book *Amazing Grace* by Mary Hoffman, copies of "All About You" activity sheet (page 29), and pens, pencils, or markers

LESSON PLAN

READ *Amazing Grace*. When the teacher announces a classroom production of *Peter Pan*, Grace wants to play the lead. She becomes discouraged when a classmate says she can't be the lead because she's a girl.

DISCUSS How did Grace feel when she first found out about the play? How did some of her classmates treat her? What did Grace learn about celebrating her uniqueness? What did her classmates learn about accepting each other and treating others with respect? Review the golden rule and relate it to the story.

DO the "All About You" activity sheet. Ask students to complete the activity with a partner. Students take turns interviewing each other to complete the activity sheet.

RELATE to daily life by having students share in the large group what they learned about each other. Ask them what it means to be unique. Discuss the importance of uniqueness. Invite the children to brainstorm different ways that each of them is unique. (Include: where they come from, the way they look or sound, things they like to do, books they like to read, hobbies and interests they have.) You may also want to create a "We Are All Unique" classroom book. Have students write a short story about how they are unique or how the person they interviewed is unique.

You and Me

LEARNING OBJECTIVES

Students will:

- compare similarities and differences among themselves and their classmates
- learn that everyone deserves to feel included, regardless of their differences

MATERIALS NEEDED

The book *What I Like About Me* by Allia Zobel-Nolan, copies of "You & Me" activity sheet (page 30), and pens, pencils, or markers

LESSON PLAN

READ   *What I Like About Me*. The kids in this book are as different as night and day. Some adore the fact that their braces dazzle and gleam, others feel distinguished when they wear their glasses. The best part is, they love their individuality.

An optional book for older students is *Freckle Juice* by Judy Blume. (It could take several days to complete reading the book.) Andrew wants freckles more than anything else, so Sharon offers to sell him her secret freckle recipe. Unfortunately, Andrew turns green from the recipe. Why did Andrew wish he had freckles? Have you ever wanted to be like someone else? Did Sharon treat Andrew in a respectful way? What did Andrew learn by the end of the story?

DISCUSS   the similarities and differences of the kids and how everyone deserves to feel included for who they are. It's important for students to accept themselves before they can learn how to accept others.

DO   the "You & Me" activity sheet. Have students work in teams of two to complete the activity. Encourage students to pay attention to the details of each other's outside appearance, such as hair color or style, freckles, shape of nose, glasses, and eye color.

RELATE   this activity to classroom life by having students share what they discovered about each other. Ask students if we are more alike than different? Understanding our differences helps us get along. It makes our world a more interesting place. Emphasize that part of getting to know others is recognizing similarities and differences other than outside appearance (for example, likes and dislikes, things they look for in a friend, beliefs, and family traditions).

My Family

LEARNING OBJECTIVES

Students will:

- explore what family means to them and share some important things they learned in the context of their families
- discover and learn to appreciate diversity in families

MATERIALS NEEDED

The book *Celebrating Families* by Rosmarie Hausherr, "My Family" activity sheet (page 31), and pens, pencils, or markers

LESSON PLAN

READ   *Celebrating Families*. This book presents a visual cross-section of real children, their families, and life in America.

DISCUSS   the importance of being part of a family and knowing that your family cares about you. Ask students about their families: How many members are there? Who are they? What do you usually do together? What do you like to celebrate? What makes your family special? What have you learned from your parents, grandparents, or elders in your family?

DO   the "My Family" activity sheet. Children from stepfamilies, adoptive families, or foster families may need guidance and support to complete the activity. Encourage them to focus on their stepfamily or adoptive or foster family.

RELATE   to daily life by discussing family similarities and differences. Ask each child to refer to the activity sheet to share one thing he or she appreciates about his or her family.

For further class discussion, read *Families Are Forever* by Craig Shemin. In this heartwarming tale of family love and beginnings, Rain meets Bo and her new "forever" mom, and they become a new family.

My Positive Traits

(You may want to use this activity along with the following activity, "Ambassadors of Peace.")

LEARNING OBJECTIVES

Students will:

- define positive character and identify individual character strengths that benefit their classroom community
- recognize and celebrate their uniqueness and their heritage

MATERIALS NEEDED

The book *The Name Jar* by Yangsook Choi, "My Positive Traits" activity sheet (page 32), scissors, glue, and pens, pencils, or markers

LESSON PLAN

READ   *The Name Jar.* Unhei and her family have just moved from Korea to the United States. Unhei is starting school. Her name is pronounced Yoon-hye, which means *grace,* but she feels awkward after some students tease her about it on the school bus. She wants an American name, and her classmates help her choose one.

DISCUSS   Why was Unhei so unhappy when she started school? What did she wish for? How did her classmates try to help? What did she finally decide to do after a talk with her mother?

DO   Review the meaning of *uniqueness* and why it is important to accept who we are as individuals. Have students complete the "My Positive Traits" activity sheet. Students will identify their positive character traits/strengths and write them in the spaces provided. Have students cut out the trait labels and glue them to the body.

RELATE   the activity to your students' lives by discussing what character is and why character is important. Ask: How do positive character traits help us get along? What positive characteristics did you choose on the activity sheet? Where do we learn how to develop positive character traits? What have you learned from your families about accepting individuality?

Collect the labeled bodies to use with the following "Ambassadors of Peace" activity.

Ambassadors of Peace

(Use this activity in combination with the previous "My Positive Traits" activity. The positive character traits are the foundation for becoming an Ambassador of Peace.)

LEARNING OBJECTIVES

Students will:

- explore what an Ambassador of Peace is and how they can become ambassadors
- write a want ad describing the job of an Ambassador of Peace

MATERIALS NEEDED

The book *Peace Begins with You* by Katherine Scholes, "Ambassadors of Peace" activity sheet (page 33), and pencils or pens

LESSON PLAN

READ   *Peace Begins with You.* The book empowers children by suggesting steps they can take to become peacemakers. It includes discussion ideas for teachers.

DISCUSS   What is an Ambassadors of Peace? Who can become an Ambassador of Peace and how? How do positive character traits (refer to completed "My Positive Traits" activity sheets) help us become Ambassadors of Peace?

DO   the "Ambassadors of Peace" activity sheet.

RELATE   to everyday life at school by reviewing the completed activity sheets as a group. Discuss the want ads the children wrote. Have the students describe the positive characteristics they are looking for in an Ambassador of Peace.

Me and My Safe & Caring School Quiz

To assess student progress, use the quiz on page 34. *(Answers: 1-F, 2-T, 3-F, 4-F, 5-F, 6-d, 7-c, 8-a, 9-differences, 10-pledge)*

Safe & Caring Vocabulary

Use the code to spell the missing words.

a	b	c	d	e	f	g	h	i	j	k	l	m	n	o	p	q	r	s	t	u	v	w	x	y	z

In our _ _ _ _ and _ _ _ _ _ _ _ _ _ _ _ _ _, our

_ has _ _ _ _ _ to

help us _ _ _ _ _ _ _ _. The most _ _ _ _ _ _ _ _ _ _

rule is to treat _ _ _ _ _ _ _ the way we want to

be treated, with _ _ _ _ _ _ _. We all have ways

that we are _ _ _ _ _ _ _ _ and _ _ _ _ _ _ _ _ _ _ _.

To make our school a _ _ _ place to _ _ _ _ _, we

_ _ _ _ _ _ _ to help everyone feel like they _ _ _ _ _ _.

Define the word **community**. _____

_____

_____

Use the words **respect** and **rules** in a sentence. _____

_____

we are
a safe
& caring
school.

SaFE & CaRiNG WORD FIND

Find and circle the words listed at the bottom of the page.

(Hint: Answers can run forward, backward, up, down, or diagonally.)

H	P	C	O	M	M	M	U	N	I	T	Y	G
O	E	A	F	G	N	N	Z	Q	T	K	E	E
R	U	L	E	S	B	I	E	D	S	L	T	A
P	T	A	P	C	A	Q	H	N	J	P	A	
J	C	Q	U	H	O	U	U	I	P	X	L	O
X	E	A	U	O	I	E	M	O	R	P	O	N
R	P	U	H	O	A	G	O	L	O	E	N	G
O	S	C	P	L	S	B	O	N	M	Y	T	G
G	E	Y	D	I	V	E	R	S	I	T	Y	Y
O	R	A	L	I	M	I	S	U	S	O	D	D
L	O	U	P	N	P	U	S	A	E	D	I	I
D	Z	O	C	U	L	P	A	K	V	B	F	
E	B	S	A	F	E	O	L	U	X	Z	F	
N	N	T	R	O	D	U	C	E	N	Q	E	
R	U	G	I	P	G	A	U	P	A	V	R	
U	X	O	N	B	E	L	O	N	G	R	E	
L	L	F	G	P	U	I	B	Q	D	E	N	
E	R	V	C	L	P	E	A	C	E	R	T	

SAFE CARING DIVERSITY RULES SCHOOL CLASSROOM COMMUNITY BELONG PROMISE UNIQUE GET ALONG GOLDEN RULE RESPECT PEACE SIMILAR DIFFERENT

we are
a safe
& caring
school.

SAFE & CARING PROMISE

We, the undersigned, do hereby promise to ourselves and everyone here, to do our best to follow the rules, be respectful, and make

a Safe & Caring School.

Student Signatures

_____   _____

_____   _____

_____   _____

_____   _____

_____   _____

_____   _____

_____   _____

_____   _____

_____   _____

_____

Teacher(s)

we aRe a SaFe & CaRiNG SCHOOL.

SAFE & CARING RULES

We all have the right to:

- ✔ be safe.
- ✔ be treated with respect.
- ✔ be bully free.
- ✔ share our feelings and ideas.
- ✔ agree to disagree.
- ✔ ask for help.
- ✔ learn.

we are a safe & caring school.

GOLDEN RULE

Treat others
the way you
want to be
treated...

...with
respect!

WE ARE
A SAFE
& CARING
SCHOOL.

When we use the **Golden Rule**, we show respect for others.

THE GOLDEN RULE

Solve the math problems below and use the key to decode a secret word that shows us a great way to get along with others.

corresponding letter from key

$9 + 9 =$ _____ (_____)

$15 \div 3 =$ _____ (_____)

$26 - 7 =$ _____ (_____)

$2 \times 8 =$ _____ (_____)

$10 \div 2 =$ _____ (_____)

$24 - 21 =$ _____ (_____)

$10 \times 2 =$ _____ (_____)

Draw a way you can show respect to others.

Key:

a	b	c	d	e	f	g	h	i	j	k	l	m	n	o	p	q	r	s	t	u	v	w	x	y	z
1	2	3	4	5	6	7	8	9	10	11	12	13	14	15	16	17	18	19	20	21	22	23	24	25	26

Now use the secret word in a sentence.

_____

_____

_____

My Story About Why **Respect** Is Important

_____

_____

_____

_____

_____

_____

we are a safe & caring school.

MY SAFE & CARING SCHOOL

Inclusion is a big word! It's also very important in a safe and caring school.

A safe and caring school **looks** like...

_____

_____

_____

_____

Define **inclusion**:

_____

_____

_____

_____

A safe and caring school **sounds** like...

_____

_____

_____

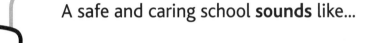

A safe and caring school **feels** like...

_____

_____

_____

_____

Can you name three things we can do to make sure everyone is included at our school?

1 -

2 -

3

we are a safe & caring school.

SEPTEMBER

OUR CLASSROOM COMMUNITY

How is your classroom like a community?

Hmm... that's a good question!

List five ways your class is like a community.

_____
_____
_____
_____
_____

Communities and classrooms both need rules to keep things running smoothly. What are some of the school rules that help everyone get along?

_____
_____
_____
_____

Now, match the beginning of each sentence below with its ending to see how our classroom is a safe and caring community.

Draw lines to show the match-ups

Our classroom community...

...everyone in our class.

We try hard to include...

...we have a caring place to learn and grow.

We can share our feelings because...

...place where everyone is accepted for who they are.

Kids and adults need a safe, fun...

...is respectful.

we ARe a saFe & CARiNG SCHOOL.

ALL ABOUT YOU

Family

Paste or draw your picture here

Friends

Our School

Our Teacher

Something I can learn at school to help the world...

Our World

Our world needs more...

we are a safe & caring school.

Favorites

Foods

Books

Movies

Music

Other

YOU
&
Me

	Similarities	Differences
Appearance • Hair • Eyes • Height		
Personality		
Culture and heritage		
Family traditions		
Favorite things we like to do		
Skills and talents		
Things we want to do when we get older		

we are
a safe
& caring
school.

My Family

Members

Family

Family is...

Holidays and traditions my family celebrates
Draw and/or write about your family traditions.

Fun things my family does together

Draw pictures and write in the circles at right to describe fun things your family does together. Then cut out the circles and string them together to create an ornament or wall-hanging.

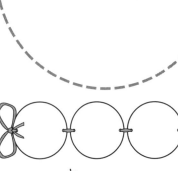

MY POSITIVE TRAITS

We all have qualities and positive traits that make us unique.

Decorate the figure to represent you. Write your best qualities on the circles. Cut out all pieces and string them together to create your personal, positive-trait mobile.

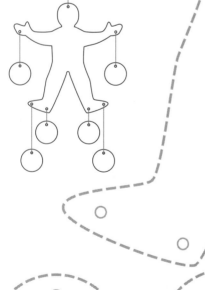

WE ARE a SAFE & CARiNG SCHOOL.

AMBASSADORS OF PEACE

Ambassadors of Peace are people who...

_____
_____
_____
_____
_____
_____

Ambassadors of Peace are cool because...

_____
_____
_____
_____
_____
_____

Write three words you would use to describe an Ambassador of Peace and use each word in a sentence.

1) _____ _____
_____
_____
_____

2) _____ _____
_____
_____
_____

3) _____ _____
_____
_____

Write a Want Ad to find an Ambassador of Peace

WANTED
Ambassador of Peace

_____
_____
_____
_____
_____
_____

we aRe
a saFe
& CaRiNG
SCHOOL.

Me and my
Safe & Caring School Quiz

True or False (circle the correct answer)

1) It really is not very important that we get to know others in our classroom community. .... **True / False**

2) We can all work together to write rules that help us get along. .... **True / False**

3) If everyone at school is unique, then we can't have anything in common. .... **True / False**

4) To get people to respect you, make sure they know not to mess with you. .... **True / False**

5) It will be just fine if I don't include everyone. Besides, we can't all do the
same thing anyway. .... **True / False**

Multiple Choice (circle the correct answer)

6) In a Safe & Caring School:

   a. everyone has the right to be safe.

   b. we accept each other for who we are.

   c. we learn how to share feelings in positive ways.

   d. all of the above.

7) The opposite of exclusion is:

   a. giving someone a hard time.

   b. ignoring somebody because they are different.

   c. the whole group working together.

   d. crossing someone off your list.

8) Ambassadors of Peace help make our school Safe & Caring by:

   a. setting a good example.

   b. having a negative attitude.

   c. tattling on everyone they don't like.

   d. being too cool to care.

Fill in the Blanks

9) We all have similarities and **d**_____.

10) Our Safe & Caring promise is a **p**_____that we will work together to have
a great school year.

Real-Life Writing

A new student joins your classroom. Describe to the newcomer why we pledge to be a Safe
and Caring School and how our classroom community creates a great place to learn and grow.

we are
a safe
& caring
school.

OCTOBER
Discovering Our Feelings

- **Awareness and Appropriate Expression of Feelings**
- **Anger Management**

- **Problem Solving**
- **Assertiveness**

Empathy (recognizing and understanding other's feelings) and the ability to communicate effectively are key qualities children need in order to get along with others. Before we teach them to be assertive, they should recognize the causes and effects of negative attitudes and behaviors. They need to realize they have the power to choose how to respond to conflict. Being "emotionally fit" helps children face daily challenges in positive ways.

MONTHLY OBJECTIVES
Students will:

- identify and express their feelings appropriately through interactive activities and role play
- learn two strategies—"I-Messages" and "Stop, Think, Choose"—to help them resolve conflicts in positive ways

TEACHING TIPS

- One of the greatest gifts we can give children is a sense of belonging. You can develop a trusting relationship with your students by getting to know them. Provide them opportunities to share something about their life in group meeting time. No matter how insignificant something might sound to you, it may be of great importance to a child.

- Use group meeting time to encourage students to share something about their lives. Have students toss a ball to one another, asking the child with the ball, "What's new in your life this week?" This is a nice way to start each day, and it lets kids know how much their lives and feelings matter to you.

OCTOBER INTEGRATED ACTIVITIES

In addition to the specific lesson plans for this month, you can use these optional ideas to integrate and extend the Safe & Caring themes into your daily routines and across the curricular areas.

LANGUAGE ARTS

- Select a book on feelings, such as *Feelings* by Aliki. After students read the book, have them write how the characters felt, why they felt that way, and how they chose to express their emotions.

- Have older students visit the primary grades to read picture books about feelings. (For example, *The Way I Feel* by Janan Cain or *When Sophie Gets Angry…Really, Really Angry* by Molly Bang.)

- Ask students to create a skit or puppet show about feelings, and have a performance for younger students or parents.

- Discuss an appropriate TV show students watch, or choose a movie to watch in class. Ask students to write or draw the characters' emotions.

LITERATURE

- Have students visit the school or local library to find books about emotions. Create book review clubs, and, once a week, have students give their expert opinions on the books they read.

- Have students create their own classroom book of short stories about feelings.

- Read *Word Wizard* by Cathryn Falwell. Anna discovers that the letters in her alphabet cereal can rearrange themselves to spell words. Divide the class into small groups and give each group three or four letters of the alphabet. Ask students to write as many feelings words as they can that start with their specific letters. When they complete their lists, have all groups work together to create a feelings dictionary.

SOCIAL STUDIES

- Have students design a school bulletin board using words and pictures that describe different feelings.

- Compare different cultures' traditions, beliefs, customs, music, food, or other characteristics. Explore how each culture expresses emotions.

ART

- Read *How Are You Peeling? Food with Moods* by Saxton Freymann, a fun book that illustrates emotions with food. Children will enjoy creating posters that show their own food emotions.

- Create self-portraits showing emotions. Talk about appropriate ways to express these feelings.

- *C Is for Curious, an ABC of Feelings* by Woodleigh Hubbard is fun to read prior to creating a picture dictionary of feelings. Have each student draw a specific feeling next to a feeling word. Compile the artwork into a dictionary of feelings.

- Read *Today I Feel Silly & Other Moods that Make My Day* by Jamie Lee Curtis. Then discuss times when students had different moods, even on the same day. Have them create self-portraits that show their favorite or least favorite moods.

MUSIC

- Play different songs and ask students to identify the moods and emotions in each song. Great songs can be found on *Children's Songs for Peace and a Better World* by The Mosaic Project.

- Provide students the opportunity to listen to different genres of music and discuss the different emotions the music evokes.

- Ask students to bring songs they like. Discuss what emotions they feel as they listen to the music. How do the rhythm, words, and melodies affect how a song makes us feel?

MATH

- Have students tally the emotions they see in their classroom each day. At the end of the week, create graphs of the number of emotions they witnessed.

- After collecting data on the emotions of classmates for a period of time, have students identify the rate of emotional responses using the math terms *most, least, greatest, lowest, average, mean.*

Safe & Caring Vocabulary and Word Find

LEARNING OBJECTIVES

Students will:

- be introduced to vocabulary that supports learning about their feelings and understanding how they relate to their safe and caring classroom
- internalize the vocabulary as they use it throughout the month and year in real life situations

MATERIALS NEEDED

"Safe & Caring Vocabulary" (page 42) and "Safe & Caring Word Find" (page 43) activity sheets, dictionaries, pencils

LESSON PLAN

Use the vocabulary activities to introduce the concepts and common language associated with this month's theme. Throughout the month, use the words in writing, spelling, storytelling, and dealing with conflict situations.

For "Safe & Caring Schools Vocabulary," explain how to choose the correct word from the word bank to decipher the message. (We all have *feelings*. Some of our feelings make us *uncomfortable*, but they are all *important*. Sometimes so many *changes* happen in our lives that it can be *stressful*. To help us stay *healthy*, we need to *learn* how to *calm down* and *share* our feelings in a *respectful* way. One *positive* way to share how you feel is to use *I-messages*.)

For "Safe & Caring Word Find," discuss what the words mean after completing the page. You may want students to work in pairs to help each other.

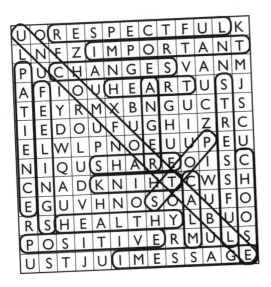

Feelings Smoothie

LEARNING OBJECTIVES

Students will:

- learn to identify their feelings and emotions and how they feel in different situations
- understand the importance of expressing their feelings in a respectful way

MATERIALS NEEDED

The book *A to Z: Do You Ever Feel Like Me?* by Bonnie Hausman and Sandi Fellman, copies of the "Feelings Smoothie" activity sheet (page 44), and pens, pencils, or markers

LESSON PLAN

READ   *A to Z: Do You Ever Feel Like Me?* Even though this book is for younger children, your students will enjoy it, too. Let them know you want them to have fun exploring situations in which they have different kinds of feelings.

DISCUSS   the different feelings people have. Feelings are an important part of who we are. We have feelings about the different things that happen to us every day. Sometimes we like the way we feel, and sometimes we don't, especially when we feel mad, sad, scared, or embarrassed. Help students make a list of different feelings. Explain that all our feelings are important, but sometimes we're not sure which words express how we feel. When our feelings get mixed up, it may be hard to say the right thing. Emphasize that if we learn to share our feelings in a caring way, we can get along better with our friends.

DO   the "Feelings Smoothie" activity sheet, having students unscramble the feelings words.

RELATE   the lesson to daily life by reviewing with students how many feelings words they discovered. Tally how many students have felt each feeling. Remind them how important it is to share their feelings in a respectful way.

How Do You Feel?

LEARNING OBJECTIVES

Students will:

- learn how to match facial expressions with different emotions
- explore how different situations make them feel

MATERIALS NEEDED

The book *The Boys' & Girls' Book of Dealing with Feelings* by Eric Dlugokinski, "How Do You Feel?" activity sheet (page 45), and pens, pencils, or markers

LESSON PLAN

READ   *The Boys' & Girls' Book of Dealing with Feelings*. This book is a good review of different emotions and how to express them in appropriate ways.

DISCUSS   the feelings presented in the book and the ways students can match feelings with facial expressions. Involve the students in using facial expressions to show how they feel. See if they can predict how others are feeling just by looking at their expressions. Have children predict what feelings they might have in different situations.

DO   the "How Do You Feel?" activity sheet.

RELATE   today's topic to the kids' lives by asking them to share their activity sheet responses with their classmates. Give students the right to pass if they feel uncomfortable sharing feelings.

What Can I Do When I Get Angry?

LEARNING OBJECTIVES

Students will:

- gain a better understanding of what happens to their bodies when they feel angry
- learn positive ways to transition from anger to calmness

MATERIALS NEEDED

The book *Dealing with Anger* by Marianne Johnston, "What Can I Do When I'm Really Angry?" activity sheet (page 46), and pens, pencils, or markers

LESSON PLAN

READ   *Dealing with Anger*. This book gives examples of different kinds of anger and offers suggestions on how to deal with anger in different situations.

As an option, read *A Volcano in My Tummy* by Eliane Whitehouse and Warwick Pudney. This book helps 6- to 15-year-olds handle their anger so they can live successful, healthy, happy, and nonviolent lives.

DISCUSS   the negative and positive ways people express their anger. Remind students that all feelings are important, but it is never okay to hurt others when you are angry.

DO   the "What Can I Do When I'm Really Angry?" activity sheet. The activity sheet illustrates how our bodies

sometimes react to anger. In small groups, have the students discuss other possible signs of anger and then make a list of positive choices to make so you can let go of anger and calm down. As a class, review the signs of anger and the positive choices the students named. Have the children name their favorite choice to help them calm down.

RELATE   the lesson to playing on the playground by having the students share specific choices they have made to calm down when they are angry.

The Anger Meter

LEARNING OBJECTIVES

Students will:

- identify different degrees of anger
- discover they have the power to choose how they respond to their anger

MATERIALS NEEDED

The book *Is It Right to Fight?* by Pat Thomas, "The Anger Meter" activity sheet (page 47), and pens, pencils, or markers

LESSON PLAN

READ   *Is It Right to Fight?* This book describes situations when children feel upset, angry, or frustrated with those around them. The students will learn that it is okay to feel frustrated or angry as long as they choose to resolve their problems in peaceful ways.

As an optional reading choice for classroom shared or modeled reading, consider *Judy Moody* by Megan McDonald. A third-grade girl is crabby and having a hard first day of school until she gets an assignment to create a collage all about herself.

DISCUSS   how we can recognize our anger level in different situations. What choices can we make when feeling angry? Explain that everyone responds to situations in different ways. One student may feel frustrated when someone cuts in line, but another student may feel very angry about the same thing.

DO   the "Anger Meter" activity sheet.

RELATE   this activity to daily life by asking students to share completed activity sheets in class. Point out the similarities and differences in how students felt and reacted in different situations. Have the students give examples of times they recognized and respected other's feelings. What suggestions do they have for resolving conflicts in positive ways?

Stop, Think, Choose

LEARNING OBJECTIVES

Students will:

- review different emotions, especially negative ones
- learn a simple process to help them stay calm and resolve conflicts in a positive way

MATERIALS NEEDED

The book *Feelings* by Aliki, "Stop, Think, Choose" miniposter (page 48), and colored pencils, crayons, or markers

LESSON PLAN

READ   *Feelings*. This book comprehensively reviews feelings and ways to express emotions appropriately. You may want to highlight certain feelings, particularly anger, as you read.

DISCUSS   Show students the "Stop, Think, Choose" miniposter, or use the large laminated poster, if you have it. Discuss the uses of a stoplight on the street, and explain that the colors on this stoplight are to remind them to *Stop* (red), *Think* (yellow), and *Choose* (green).

DO   Have students color the words on their miniposters using red, yellow, and green markers, crayons, or pencils. Ask older students to prepare their miniposters for teaching this skill to younger students in the school. You also could have your students prepare the posters for display throughout the school.

Explain that the kids can use Stop, Think, Choose to help them stay calm when they are angry or having a conflict with someone. Teach these steps:

- Stop (red): When angry, slow down, breathe, and relax.
- Think (yellow): Ask yourself, what's the problem? How am I feeling? How is the other person feeling? What are my options for solving the problem? What can I do about it? What will be the consequences of my choice?
- Choose (green): Use safe and caring words. Make a good choice about what to do.

RELATE   Practice using Stop, Think, Choose by role-playing the following situations:

- Inclusion. A group of children is playing a game at recess and they do not want to include you. What do you do? (Stop, Think, Choose)
- Taking Turns. You are waiting for your turn on the swing, but your friend won't get off. What do you do? (Stop, Think, Choose)
- Sharing. It is time to choose a book for quiet reading time, but someone else wants to read the same book as you. What do you do? (Stop, Think, Choose)
- Rejection. Your friend says that he or she does not want to go to the movies with you. What do you do? (Stop, Think, Choose)
- Respecting Property. Someone takes something from your desk without asking. What do you do? (Stop, Think, Choose)

Remind the students that they can always ask for help from people they know and trust if they cannot solve a problem by themselves.

I-Messages

LEARNING OBJECTIVES

Students will:

- learn to use "I-messages" to help them express how they feel in a positive way during conflicts
- practice using I-messages to communicate how they feel during conflict without blaming others

MATERIALS NEEDED

The book *Learning About Assertiveness from the Life of Oprah Winfrey* by Kristin Ward, "I-Messages" activity sheet (page 49), and pens, pencils, or markers

LESSON PLAN

READ   *Learning About Assertiveness from the Life of Oprah Winfrey*. Oprah Winfrey explains why assertiveness is important and how it helped in her personal and professional life.

DISCUSS   How did being assertive help Oprah? What did she do that you would consider being assertive? Discuss how sometimes people hurt our feelings without knowing they did. How do you say how you feel in a respectful way when you are upset with a friend, or when there is a problem?

DO Use the "I-Messages" steps to practice communicating feelings when there is a problem or disagreement: I feel _____ when you_____. I need _____. After students have an understanding of the process, distribute the "I-Message" activity sheets and have students complete their own I-message.

Ask students to relate I-messages to what Oprah did. What kind of I-message might Oprah have used?

RELATE the activity to daily life at school by encouraging the students to use I-messages. Explain that it may take time to remember how to use I-messages, but they will likely have many opportunities to practice. They can refer often to the "I-Messages" activity sheets for a reminder of the steps. As you read books dealing with conflict, encourage children to help the characters in the books use I-messages to resolve their conflicts.

Feelings and Actions

LEARNING OBJECTIVES
Students will:

- learn how to use Stop, Think, Choose in combination with I-messages to help solve problems
- predict and identify the consequences of their choices

MATERIALS NEEDED

The book *How to Take the Grrrr Out of Anger* by Elizabeth Verdick and Marjorie Lisovskis, "Feelings and Actions" activity sheet (page 50), and pens or pencils

LESSON PLAN

READ *How to Take the Grrrr Out of Anger*, especially "Chapter 7: Six Steps to Solving Anger Problems." Blending tips and ideas with jokes and funny cartoons, this book helps kids understand that anger is normal and can be expressed in many ways.

DISCUSS What is the definition of *anger*? In what ways have you seen anger expressed? Ask students to create a list of daily challenges they face at school, at home, and in the neighborhood.

DO the "Feelings and Actions" activity sheet. Have students pick one situation from the list of challenges they face at school to complete the activity.

RELATE the activity to everyday life by going over the completed activity sheets as a group. Discuss the connection between feelings, thoughts, and actions. Review how to predict what might happen if they choose to behave in

negative versus positive ways. Practice using Stop, Think, Choose and I-messages in actual situations at school.

Patience Please

LEARNING OBJECTIVES
Students will:

- understand what it means to be patient
- learn specific steps they can take to learn how to be more patient

MATERIALS NEEDED

The book *I Can't Wait* by Elizabeth Crary, "Patience Please!" activity sheet (page 51), and pens or pencils

LESSON PLAN

READ *I Can't Wait*. Luke wants his turn on the tumbling mat now! What can he do?

DISCUSS Ask students to define the word *patience*. Why do we need to be patient? Review some of the problem-solving ideas found in the book.

DO the "Patience Please!" activity sheet.

RELATE topics from the activity sheets to the kids' daily activities. When is it hard to be patient? What happens when we are patient compared to being impatient? Use classroom scenarios to provide discussion. For example, your classmate has five minutes left in her computer time, but you have so much work to do and need to use the computer now—what can you do? Help students make the connection between impatience and negative consequences.

Guess That Feeling

LEARNING OBJECTIVES
Students will:

- identify nonverbal behaviors associated with specific feelings and learn how to recognize how others feel in different situations
- explore the effect of their actions on other people

MATERIALS NEEDED

The book *Angel Child, Dragon Child* by Michele Maria Surat, "Guess That Feeling" activity sheet (page 52), and pens or pencils

LESSON PLAN

READ *Angel Child, Dragon Child*. Ut, a Vietnamese girl attending school in the United States, misses her mother in Vietnam. To make matters worse, Raymond, a boy in her new school teases her and pushes her around. Surprisingly, Raymond presents her with a wonderful gift to help her feel better.

> An optional reading choice for classroom shared or modeled reading is *See You Around, Sam!* by Lois Lowry. Mad at his mother, Sam Krupnik decides to run away to Alaska, but as he says his good-byes, his resolve to run away begins to wane. How did Sam's family and friends know he was upset? What advice did he get from his neighbors and friends? How did he feel by the end of the story?

DISCUSS Raymond's behavior toward Ut. Why do you think he acted that way? Did Ut's response to his bullying make it better or worse?

DO Talk with students about body language and nonverbal communication. Ask them to share examples of body language that they use or see in others. Have students complete the "Guess That Feeling" activity sheet.

RELATE the lesson to daily life at school and home. Ask why it is important for us to recognize how others feel and to respond appropriately. Have students practice, through role-play, how to recognize someone's feelings by paying attention to their facial expressions, body language, and voice. What is the connection between recognition and empathy?

What Do You Tell Yourself?

LEARNING OBJECTIVES

Students will:

- identify the difference between positive and negative self-talk

- practice using positive self-talk in difficult situations

MATERIALS NEEDED

The book *Shrinking Violet* by Cari Best, "What Do You Tell Yourself?" activity sheet (page 53), and pens or pencils

LESSON PLAN

READ *Shrinking Violet*. When Irwin taunts Violet about her fat knees and more, all she wants to do is shrink away. On opening night of the play, Irwin forgets his lines, and Violet steps in and saves the day.

DISCUSS Describe how Irwin treated Violet. How did Violet feel when she was teased? What did she do when she was alone to make herself feel better? How did she save the day?

DO Explain the difference between positive and negative self-talk and ask students to brainstorm examples of each. Distribute the "What Do You Tell Yourself?" activity sheet. Have students work in pairs to complete the activity.

RELATE the activity to daily life by reviewing the completed activity sheets. Ask: Was the positive or negative comment easier to write? Why? Why is it important to learn how to use positive self-talk? Have you ever found yourselves using negative self-talk? Discuss ways to change negative self-talk to positive self-talk.

Discovering Our Feelings Quiz

To assess student progress, use the quiz on page 54. *(Answers: 1-F, 2-T, 3-T, 4-F, 5-T, 6-b, 7-d, 8-d, 9-choice, 10-patient)*

Safe & Caring Vocabulary

Fill in the blanks below with the correct words from the list.

important	learn	share
positive	changes	feelings
stressful	calm down	uncomfortable
healthy	I-messages	respectful

We all have _ _ _ _ _ _ _ _. Some of our feelings make us _ _ _ _ _ _ _ _ _ _ _ _ _ _, but they are all _ _ _ _ _ _ _ _. Sometimes so many _ _ _ _ _ _ _ happen in our lives that it can be _ _ _ _ _ _ _ _ _. To help us stay _ _ _ _ _ _ _, we need to _ _ _ _ _ how to _ _ _ _ _ _ _ _ and _ _ _ _ _ our feelings in a _ _ _ _ _ _ _ _ _ _ way. One _ _ _ _ _ _ _ _ way to share how you feel is to use _ – _ _ _ _ _ _ _ _.

Define the word **stress.** _____

_____

_____

Write a sentence using the words **calm** and **feeling.**

_____

_____

SAFE & CARING WORD FIND

Find and circle the words listed at the bottom of the page.
(Hint: Answers can run forward, backward, up, down, or diagonally.)

U	O	R	E	S	P	E	C	T	F	U	L	K
L	N	F	Z	I	M	P	O	R	T	A	N	T
P	U	C	H	A	N	G	E	S	V	A	N	M
A	F	I	O	U	H	E	A	R	T	U	S	J
T	E	Y	R	M	X	B	N	G	U	C	T	S
I	E	D	O	U	F	U	G	H	I	Z	R	C
E	L	W	L	P	N	O	E	U	U	P	E	U
N	I	Q	U	S	H	A	R	E	O	I	S	C
C	N	A	D	K	N	I	H	T	C	W	S	H
E	G	U	V	H	N	O	S	O	A	U	F	O
R	S	H	E	A	L	T	H	Y	L	B	U	O
P	O	S	I	T	I	V	E	R	M	U	L	S
U	S	T	J	U	I	M	E	S	S	A	G	E

CHANGES	THINK	STRESSFUL	UNCOMFORTABLE
CALM	HEART	SHARE	IMPORTANT
ANGER	PATIENCE	RESPECTFUL	
STOP	POSITIVE	CHOOSE	
HEALTHY	FEELINGS	I-MESSAGE	

we are
a safe
& caring
school.

FEELINGS SMOOTHIE

We have lots of feelings. Sometimes they get all mixed up. Unscramble the feelings words in the blender and write the words on the lines in the glass below.

amd adlg
redcas nayqr
dsa
paphy
detssres
rhut
almc hsy

1 _____
2 _____
3 _____
4 _____
5 _____
6 _____
7 _____
8 _____
9 _____
10 _____

WE ARE a SaFE & CaRiNG SCHOOL.

HOW DO YOU FEEL?

Draw
how you
feel
when...

...someone teases you.

...someone invites you
to a birthday party.

...you get blamed for
something you didn't do.

...you do a great job
on a school project.

Tough Spots

Your best friend got a new bike just like the one you really wanted.

How do you feel?_____

What can you do? _____

You want to join a game during recess, but the other kids won't let you.

How do you feel?_____

What can you do?_____

Your friend loaned you a favorite sweatshirt and you lost it.

How do you feel? _____

What can you do? _____

we aRe
a saFe
& CaRiNG
SCHOOL.

WHAT CAN I DO WHEN I'M REALLY ANGRY?

When I get angry...

- my hands turn into fists
- my eyes hurt
- my face feels hot
- I get a headache
- my stomach hurts
- I get sweaty

List things you can do to help yourself when you feel angry, and then describe what works best, and why.

My list of things to do when I get angry:

	I do this alone	With someone

From the list above, what works best to help you calm down, and why?

we are
a safe
& caring
school.

The Anger Meter

Okay ① Frustrated ② Upset ③ Angry ④ Furious! ⑤

Write a number from 1 to 5 in the Anger Meters to describe how you might feel in the following situations.

If someone made fun of the way you look, how would you feel?
_____

If someone called you a name, how would you feel?
_____

If someone took your things without asking, how would you feel?
_____

If someone cut in line in front of you, how would you feel?
_____

If someone spread rumors about you, how would you feel?
_____

If someone teased you about a new haircut, how would you feel?
_____

Other?
_____

How would you feel?

_____

_____

we are a safe & caring school.

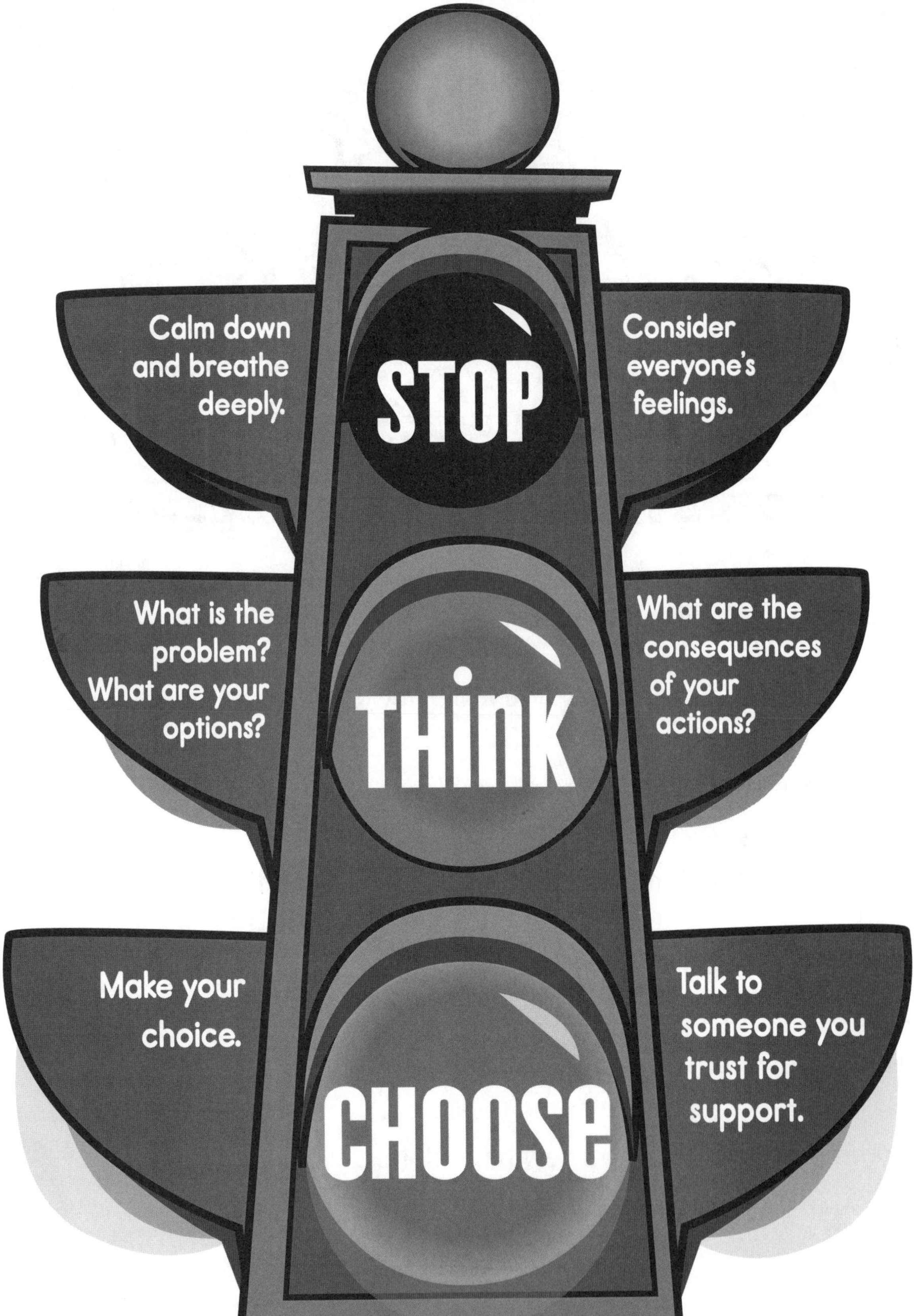

Calm down and breathe deeply.

Consider everyone's feelings.

STOP

What is the problem? What are your options?

What are the consequences of your actions?

THINK

Make your choice.

Talk to someone you trust for support.

CHOOSE

we are
a safe
& caring
SCHOOL.

I-Messages

When you're in a tough spot, you can use **I-Messages** to help figure out a good solution. Follow the steps below.

1) I feel...(write how you feel)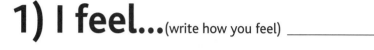

_____

_____

_____

_____

_____

2) When...(write what happened)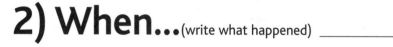

_____

_____

_____

_____

_____

3) I need...(write what you need to make things better)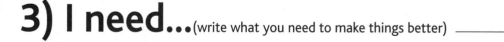

_____

_____

_____

_____

we are
a safe
& caring
school.

Feelings and actions

We face challenges better when we connect our feelings and our actions.

Stop

I feel _____

when _____

_____

_____

_____

_____

Think

What are the options and likely consequences of my choices?

If I do this...

Then this will happen...

Because...

Choose

Think of a problem and use **Stop, Think, Choose** to make the best choice.

I can make things better by

_____

_____

_____

Remember, using **Stop, Think, Choose** and **I-messages** really help you communicate better!

WE ARE
A SAFE
& CARING
SCHOOL.

Patience Please!

Write three things you sometimes have to wait for. Then rate if it is easy or hard to wait for them.

1

HELP! ⬤○○○○ No Problem

2

HELP! ⬤○○○○ No Problem

3

HELP! ⬤○○○○ No Problem

Can't wait? Sometimes you have to! Most of the time it's easy, but other times it's a real test of your patience.

Draw a line to show which is the appropriate column for each word.

Patient   Impatient

grouchy
calm
pushy
rude
quiet
pacing
polite
helpful
fidgety

What can you do when it's hard to wait? Try these ideas!

Do something different while you wait. Like what?

_____

_____

Stay calm. How?

_____

_____

Write a story about a time when you had to wait. How did you feel? What did you do to pass the time?

_____

_____

_____

_____

We are a safe & caring school.

OCTOBER

GUESS THAT FEELING

Everybody's feelings are important. But how can we tell how another person feels? Try paying attention to three things . . .

1. Face
2. Body Language
3. Voice

Imagine how your friends might feel in each of the situations below. Draw or write what you think your friend's face, body language, and voice might look or sound like. Finally, tell what your friend is feeling.

Situation	Face	Body Language	Voice	What are they feeling?
Your friend's bike was stolen.				
A classmate was teased about her new glasses.				
Your friend got a prize for doing a great job on a test.				
You told your best friend that you're moving away.				

WE ARE
A SAFE
& CARING
SCHOOL.

WHAT DO YOU TELL YOURSELF?

When you find yourself in a tough spot, do you tell yourself positive things or negative things?

What do you mean?

Things we choose to tell ourselves can help us calm down and feel better about a situation, or they can upset us more.

Think about how you might feel and what you might tell yourself in the following situations. Draw a face that shows how you feel and write a positive and a negative comment.

You're trying out for a team.

I'm a good player, and this year I'm going to try my very hardest to make the team!

I'm no good, so I'll never get picked for the team. I don't really care anyway.

You're taking a tough science test.

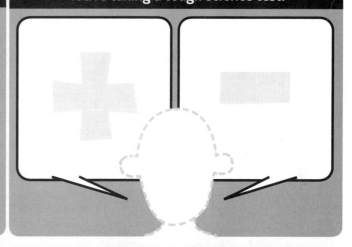

You just got teased about your new haircut.

You're giving a speech in front of the class.

we ARe a saFe & CaRiNG SCHOOL.

DISCOVERING OUR FEELINGS QUIZ

True or False (circle the correct answer)

1) Only my feelings are important. . . . . **True / False**

2) We all have many different feelings . . . . **True / False**

3) Sometimes we do not know what to do with our feelings and it helps
to talk with someone . . . . **True / False**

4) When someone does not care about your feelings, you do not have to care about
his or her feelings . . . . **True / False**

5) We can get along much better when we care how each other person feels . . . . **True / False**

Multiple Choice (circle the correct answer)

6) When you are angry:
- **a.** there is nothing you can do about it.
- **b.** it is wise to use positive ways to calm down.
- **c.** it helps to be mean to others.
- **d.** nobody cares how you feel.

7) Stop, Think, Choose helps us:
- **a.** calm down when there is a problem.
- **b.** consider everyone's feelings, including our own.
- **c.** choose the best way to solve a problem.
- **d.** all of the above.

8) To understand how others feel:
- **a.** just guess because it is too hard to know.
- **b.** listen to their voice.
- **c.** watch their body language and face.
- **d.** b and c.

Fill in the Blanks

9) Use Stop, Think, Choose to help make the best **c**_____.

10) It is easier to wait when we know how to be **p**_____.

Real-Life Writing
You had a tough time on a test that you thought would be easy. Write what you can tell yourself
so you feel better and do better next time.

NOVEMBER
My Support System

- **Creating a Support System**
- **Asking for Help**
- **Friendship**
- **Appreciation**

It is essential that we recognize and take seriously the stress in children's lives. Today, students worry about family issues, friends, academic performance, peer pressure, and much more. We can model healthy ways of dealing with stress and create a support system where children can practice asking for help appropriately.

MONTHLY OBJECTIVES
Students will:

- discuss qualities of friendship, how good friends are an important part of their support systems, and how to ask for help from people they trust
- learn to express appreciation for help they receive and to care about others
- understand that peer pressure can have a big impact on support systems

TEACHING TIPS

Creating a safe and caring school community takes time and a deliberate effort by everyone. As a staff member, support each other in your efforts to build a positive school climate. As a teacher, look for opportunities to model desirable behavior for students. Use the teachable moments to reinforce monthly themes. Integrate teaching of social and emotional skills into your daily routine.

NOVEMBER INTEGRATED ACTIVITIES

In addition to the specific lesson plans for this month, you can use these optional ideas to integrate and extend the Safe & Caring themes into your daily routines and across curricular areas.

LANGUAGE ARTS

- Have students use poems or short stories to give short presentations about best friends or the qualities of friendship.

- In small groups, have students generate two lists: top qualities of good friends and ways to make friends. Create posters using the lists and post them around the room as reminders of how to build positive friendships.

- Create a "Friendship Recipe Book." Write ideas on how to make friends in the form of a recipe. List the ingredients and the directions for a good friendship.

LITERATURE

- *Koya DeLaney* and the *Good Girl Blues* by Eloise Greenfield. Loritha and her best friend are members of the double-dutch jump-rope team. When a rift develops between them, Koya gets the blues trying to be the peacemaker.

- Have students write skits about friendship and perform them for other students.

- Encourage students to read books where characters learn how to ask for help from people they know and trust. Some books to consider are *Amazing Grace* by Mary Hoffman, *The Biggest Klutz in Fifth Grade* by Bill Wallace, *Next-Door Neighbors* by Sarah Ellis, and *Fish Face* by Patricia Reilly Giff.

- As a class, adapt a book on friendship into a "Reader's Theater" and perform it for another class.

SOCIAL STUDIES

- Have students create a map of the support system within their school community, complete with the names of people they can rely on for help.

- Have students explain what kind of support they get from each person in their families. Ask them what kind of help they give their family members.

- Play a friendship yarn game. Have students stand in a circle, and one person holds a ball of yarn. The person with the ball of yarn chooses someone to throw or roll the ball to, but first gives a compliment to that person. The game continues in this manner, with each person who gets the ball of yarn holding on to a piece of it before throwing it to another person. As you play, you will see a "friendship web" being created.

ART

- Have students create collages that depict qualities of friendship. Use old magazines to cut out pictures and words that best illustrate positive friendships.

- Explore the life of Frida by reading *Frida* by Jonah Winter. The book describes how Frida used painting when she was unable to play because of her illnesses. Create a friendship mural to share what was learned from the story.

- Show students how to make friendship bracelets from colored thread or string. You can find instructions in *Friendship Bracelets* by Camilla Grysk.

MUSIC

- Listen to songs about friendship, and ask students to write words they hear in the song that have to do with friendship or relationships. Good examples can be found on *Ready to Rock Kids, Volumes 1 and 2,* by Dr. Mac & Friends; and *Company of Friends* by Linda Book.

- Ask students to write new words to familiar tunes (like "Old McDonald," or "Bingo,") to honor people who support them in their school community.

MATH

- Have students create math problems using a friendship theme. For example: Maria helped Susan with homework 2 times last week for 1 hour each time, and 3 times this week for 1 hour each time. Susan helped Maria with science 4 times last week for 1 hour each time, and 3 times this week for 1 hour each time. Which girl helped the most and by how much?

Safe & Caring Vocabulary and Word Find

LEARNING OBJECTIVES

Students will:

- be introduced to the vocabulary related to support systems and learn that support systems are important in a safe and caring classroom
- internalize the vocabulary as they use it throughout the month and year in real-life situations

MATERIALS NEEDED

Copies of "Safe & Caring Vocabulary" (page 62) and "Safe & Caring Word Find" (page 63) activity sheets, pencils, dictionaries

LESSON PLAN

Use the vocabulary activities to introduce the concepts and common language associated with this month's theme. Throughout the month, use the words in writing, spelling, storytelling, and dealing with conflict situations.

For "Safe & Caring Schools Vocabulary," explain how to unscramble the words to read the message. (We can all _support_ one another to make a _safe_ and more _caring_ school. How? By respecting each other's _rights_ and _feelings_. When we _give_ our help in return for _help_ from others, we show _appreciation_. Being supportive and a good helper leads to better _relationships_ with our _family_ and _friends_.)

For "Safe & Caring Word Find," discuss what the words mean after completing the page. You may want students to work in pairs to help each other.

People I Can Count On

LEARNING OBJECTIVES

Students will:

- learn to identify their personal support systems
- identify emergency situations and learn to ask for help when they need it

MATERIALS NEEDED

The book *The Rag Coat* by Lauren Mills, "People I Can Count On" activity sheet (page 64), and pens, pencils, or markers

LESSON PLAN

READ *The Rag Coat*. Minna proudly wears her new coat made of clothing scraps to school. The other children laugh at her until she tells them the stories behind the scraps.

DISCUSS the importance of having a support system. Everyone, even grown-ups, need people who care about them. Explain that people who care about us can help us, especially when we are not sure what to do or feel sad or upset about something. Explain the difference between emergency and no emergency situations. Discuss what to do in different types of emergencies.

DO the "People I Can Count On" activity sheet. Have students complete the activity by drawing and writing about the people they can count on at home, in their neighborhood, and at school.

RELATE Remind the children that you are one of the people they can count on. Have them think of times they may need to ask for help. Assure them that asking for help is a sign of strength, not weakness.

Amazing Changes

LEARNING OBJECTIVES

Students will:

- learn to identify different changes people experience
- respond to change in positive ways

MATERIALS NEEDED

The book *Always and Forever* by Alan Durant, "Amazing Changes" activity sheet (page 65), and pens, pencils, or markers

LESSON PLAN

READ *Always and Forever.* Otter, Mole, Fox, and Hare share a house in the woods. When Fox dies, the other three struggle with their grief. By remembering the love, wisdom, and support Fox showed them and the funny things he used to do, they realize that Fox is with them "always and forever" in their memories and laughter.

DISCUSS the different kinds of changes children experience in their lives (for example, moving, changing schools, parents' divorce, a new sibling, death in family). Tell students that sometimes changes are happy, sometimes stressful, and sometimes sad. Ask them how we can be respectful of other people's feelings.

DO the "Amazing Changes" activity sheet. Have students find their way through the maze. When they come upon the changes, have them indicate whether a change is a good change or a stressful change by coloring either the happy or sad face. Then, answer the questions in the center.

RELATE the activity to the kids' daily lives by reminding them that change is a normal part of life. Ask for volunteers to share examples of changes in their lives in recent months or years. Ask how they felt about the changes.

What Is a Friend?

LEARNING OBJECTIVES

Students will:

- learn how to identify the qualities of a good friend
- practice getting along in small groups

MATERIALS NEEDED

The book *How to Be a Friend* by Laurie Krasny Brown and Marc Brown, "What Is a Friend?" activity sheet (page 66), poster board, and pens, pencils, or markers

LESSON PLAN

READ *How to Be a Friend.* This book reviews how to make friends and examines the unavoidable situations (both good and bad) that friends experience.

DISCUSS qualities that are important in a friend. Ask children for specific examples.

DO the "What Is a Friend?" activity sheet. After students finish, divide the class into small groups. Ask each group to create a poster about friendship, using the information provided on the activity sheets and any other ideas they have about friends.

RELATE what has been learned about friends by having each group taking a turn to present the posters they created. Use the posters to decorate the hallways of the school.

Recipe for a Friend

LEARNING OBJECTIVES

Students will:

- learn about shyness
- gain a better understanding of how to make and keep friends

MATERIALS NEEDED

The book *How Kids Make Friends: Secrets for Making Lots of Friends, No Matter How Shy You Are* by Lonnie Michelle, "Recipe for a Friend" activity sheet (page 67), and pens, pencils, or markers

LESSON PLAN

READ *How Kids Make Friends: Secrets for Making Lots of Friends, No Matter How Shy You Are.* This book helps children overcome shyness and teaches them how to make new friends.

DISCUSS a common concern for kids—how to make friends. Explain that it is not always easy to make friends, especially when moving to a new school or neighborhood. Help them identify different ways they can find friends. Ask students what qualities they look for in a friend and what qualities they can offer as a friend.

DO the "Recipe for a Friend" activity sheet to reflect on the previous discussion.

RELATE the entire lesson to school life by asking students to share completed activity sheets with the class. Remind the students that to keep friends, they need to treat each other with respect and demonstrate the same characteristics they look for in a friend. Reference the "Golden Rule" poster from a previous lesson (page 25).

Give and Take

LEARNING OBJECTIVES

Students will:

- understand the importance of caring about and helping others
- learn who might help in different situations

MATERIALS NEEDED

The book *How to Lose All Your Friends* by Nancy L. Carlson, "Give & Take" activity sheet (page 68), and pens, pencils, or markers

LESSON PLAN

READ *How to Lose All Your Friends*. This reverse etiquette book advises readers to never smile or share, to be a bully, to whine, to tattle, and to be a poor sport. Each "rule" offers specific examples and is illustrated with brightly colored pictures.

> Optional books for independent reading or teachers modeled reading could include the following titles: *Some Friend!* by Carol Carrick. A boy learns how much give-and-take is required in a one-sided friendship. When pushed too far, Mike realizes he will have to take a stand or lose his self-respect. *The Berenstain Bears and the Blame Game* by Stan and Jan Berenstain. Kids learn that fighting is of no use. Instead, they get to work and solve the problem.

DISCUSS the different ways good friends help one another. Helping is part of getting along. Ask: Can you think of a time when you gave or received help? How did you feel? How do you think others felt when they received help from you?

DO Help students make a list of people they usually go to for help, noting the reasons they need help. Complete the "Give & Take" activity sheet. Ask students to create their own cartoon text showing how to ask and respond to requests for help.

RELATE the activity to daily life by asking students to share their completed activity sheets with the class. Compare the similarities and differences between ways students can ask for help or give help to others. Remind the kids that in a safe and caring school everyone deserves the right to ask for help or support, and everyone deserves to get the help or support they need.

Gift from the Heart

LEARNING OBJECTIVES

Students will:

- learn about empathy and the different ways people care for others
- learn about the importance of giving from the heart

MATERIALS NEEDED

The book *The Wednesday Surprise* by Eve Bunting, "Gift from the Heart" card template (page 69), and pens, pencils, or markers

LESSON PLAN

READ *The Wednesday Surprise*. A proud granddaughter teaches her grandmother to read. Both the grandmother and granddaughter show appreciation for each other.

> An optional book for independent reading or class-room shared reading is *Attaboy, Sam!* by Lois Lowry. For his mother's birthday, Sam concocts a special perfume by combining his mother's favorite smells: his father's pipe, freshly washed hair, and babies, to name a few. When he adds tobacco leaves, his own hair, and the stuff from the baby's diapers, you can imagine the smelly results.

DISCUSS how Anna showed how much she cared about her grandmother. What was the big surprise? How did Anna's father feel about the surprise? How did Grandma feel about Anna helping her?

DO Make "Heart Cards." Have the children draw and/or write caring messages in the card for someone in their family, someone who has helped them at school, or another person who has shown a lot of love to them.

RELATE the activity to everyday life by reviewing the specific people and things the kids are grateful for. Brainstorm ways they can be thankful and caring toward others and help make their school a safe and caring place.

Stressing the Positive

LEARNING OBJECTIVES

Students will:

- learn that stress is a normal part of life
- review positive and negative ways to respond to stress

MATERIALS NEEDED

The book *Don't Pop Your Cork on Mondays!* by Adolph Moser, "Stressing the Positive" activity sheet (page 70), and pens, pencils, or markers

LESSON PLAN

READ selections from *Don't Pop Your Cork on Mondays!* This handbook explores the causes and effects of stress and offers young people practical advice for dealing with stress.

DISCUSS   What is the definition of *stress?* How does stress impact your lives? What kinds of things create stress for you? What choices can you make to deal with stress?

DO   the "Stressing the Positive" activity sheet.

RELATE   the students' answers on the activity sheets to times when they feel a lot of stress. Encourage students to seek support from parents, teachers, or others during stressful times. Remind them they do not have to solve their problems alone.

They Made Me Do It

LEARNING OBJECTIVES

Students will:

- define peer pressure and the difference between positive and negative peer pressure
- discuss what they can do to stand up to negative peer pressure

MATERIALS NEEDED

The book *It's Not My Fault!* by Nancy L. Carlson, "They Made Me Do It!" activity sheet (page 71), and pens or pencils

LESSON PLAN

READ   *It's Not My Fault!* When called to the principal's office, George is quick to blame other people for the many things that went wrong during the day, from his late arrival to the escape of some mice.

> Optional books for independent reading or teacher modeled and shared reading could include the following: *My Brother Made Me Do It* by Peg Kehret, *Standing Up to Peer Pressure: A Guide to Being True to You* by Jim Auer, and *Stick Up for Yourself!* by Gershen Kaufman, Lev Raphael, and Pamela Espeland.

DISCUSS   In small groups, have students define *peer pressure* and make a list of positive and negative peer pressure situations. Talk about the situations and the ways kids can handle them.

DO   the "They Made Me Do It!" activity sheet.

RELATE   the students' work on the activity sheets to how often they have to deal with positive or negative peer pressure at home, in their neighborhoods, and in school. Ask: What types of peer pressure, negative or positive, have you experienced? How do you choose to deal with it? What can you do to support each other?

Caring About Compassion

LEARNING OBJECTIVES

Students will:

- define compassion and identify its synonyms and antonyms
- research historical figures who were compassionate

MATERIALS NEEDED

The book *Thank You, Mr. Falker* by Patricia Polacco, "Caring About Compassion" activity sheet (page 72), pens or pencils, dictionary, thesaurus, Internet, reference materials

LESSON PLAN

READ   *Thank You, Mr. Falker*. Trisha triumphs over dyslexia in this inspiring story. Young readers struggling with learning difficulties will identify with Trisha's situation and find reassurance in her success.

DISCUSS   What difficulties did Trisha have in school? Who realized she needed help? Why did he help her? How did Mr. Falker help Tricia? How did Tricia feel about the help, and what happened after she got help?

DO   Ask students to define *compassion* and discuss ways people show compassion toward others. Create a list of historical people the students believe had compassion for others. (For example: Florence Nightingale, Martin Luther King Jr., Jimmy Carter, Mother Teresa, Dr. Jane Goodall, Abraham Lincoln, Anne Sullivan, Helen Keller, the Pope, Ghandi, or Red Cross volunteers.) Use this list for the last section of the activity page. Complete the "Caring About Compassion" activity sheet.

RELATE   the idea of compassion to real-life people and events during the next weeks by having students share their research findings of compassionate people. As a group, decide how to be compassionate at school.

Getting Help and Helping Others

LEARNING OBJECTIVES

Students will:

- define empathy and explore the relationship between empathy and caring
- identify specific ways empathy is used to help them get along with others

MATERIALS NEEDED

The book *Chicken Sunday* by Patricia Polacco, dictionary, "Getting Help and Helping Others" activity sheet (page 73), and pens or pencils

LESSON PLAN

READ   *Chicken Sunday*. Miss Eula fixes a fried chicken dinner with all the trimmings every Sunday, and Patricia and her friends are always invited to share the meal. When the children hear that Miss Eula longs for the fancy Easter bonnet in Mr. Kodinsky's hat shop, they make a plan to raise the money to buy it for her.

DISCUSS   What did Patricia and her friends do every Sunday? What did Miss Eula want for Easter? Who helped the three friends find a way to get the hat for Miss Eula? Why did they want to get her the hat?

DO   To help students understand empathy, review what they know about caring and identifying how others feel. Distribute the "Getting Help and Helping Others" activity sheet for students to complete.

RELATE   the idea of empathy to student's lives by reviewing the completed activity sheets. Ask: Why do we need empathy? How does having empathy help us get along with others? Can you always tell how someone is feeling? Do others care about the way you feel? Who have you helped in the last few weeks?

My Support System Quiz

To assess student progress, use the quiz on page 74. (*Answers: 1-T, 2-T, 3-F, 4-T, 5-T, 6-d, 7-d, 8-d, 9-compassion, 10-positive, negative*)

Safe & Caring Vocabulary

Unscramble the words to complete the sentences.

We can all _ _ _ _ _ _ _ one another to make
t r p o s p u

a _ _ _ _ and more _ _ _ _ _ _ school. How?
e f s a   r i c a n g

By respecting each other's _ _ _ _ _ _ and
s g t i h r

_ _ _ _ _ _ _ _. When we _ _ _ _ our help in
s g e e f l i n   e g v i

return for _ _ _ _ from others, we show
l e p h

_ _ _ _ _ _ _ _ _ _ _ _. Being supportive and a good
p r e c t a p i n i o a

helper leads to better _ _ _ _ _ _ _ _ _ _ _ _ _
s i l e n s t r a h i o p

with our _ _ _ _ _ _ and _ _ _ _ _ _ _.
l i f y a m   s n i f e r d

Define the word **empathy**. _____

_____

Write a sentence using the word **appreciation** or
the word **trust**. _____

_____

we are
a safe
& caring
school.

Safe & Caring WORD FIND

Find and circle the words listed at the bottom of the page.

(Hint: Answers can run forward, backward, up, down, or diagonally.)

A	P	P	R	E	C	I	A	T	I	O	N
S	G	N	I	M	H	I	O	R	C	Y	A
O	S	A	G	P	A	P	H	U	H	H	O
C	C	I	H	A	N	K	Q	S	A	X	H
O	H	O	T	T	G	O	A	T	R	K	E
M	O	H	S	H	E	F	O	A	A	T	L
M	O	P	H	Y	E	A	R	K	C	O	P
U	L	Q	G	O	T	M	G	I	T	E	F
N	V	R	I	P	F	I	A	N	E	O	U
I	Z	O	V	U	I	L	O	G	R	N	L
C	A	R	I	N	G	Y	Q	D	W	O	D
A	S	O	N	O	U	I	U	S	U	F	A
T	T	M	G	Y	W	V	A	H	O	I	D
I	R	C	O	M	P	A	S	S	I	O	N
R	E	L	A	T	I	O	N	S	H	I	P
N	S	U	P	P	O	R	T	A	L	M	A
X	S	O	J	D	E	I	Y	R	Q	G	Z
P	E	E	R	P	R	E	S	S	U	R	E

GIVING	RELATIONSHIP	RIGHTS	PEER PRESSURE
TAKING	APPRECIATION	HELPFUL	
FRIEND	STRESS	COMPASSION	
FAMILY	CHANGE	CHARACTER	
SUPPORT	EMPATHY	CARING	

we are a safe & caring SCHOOL.

People I Can Count On

Draw and name the people you can count on.

Family

Who supports me at home?

Friends

Write two ways your friends support you.

Other

Who else can I count on for help?

Why is it important to have people I can count on?

WE ARE
A SAFE
& CARING
SCHOOL.

64

amazing changes

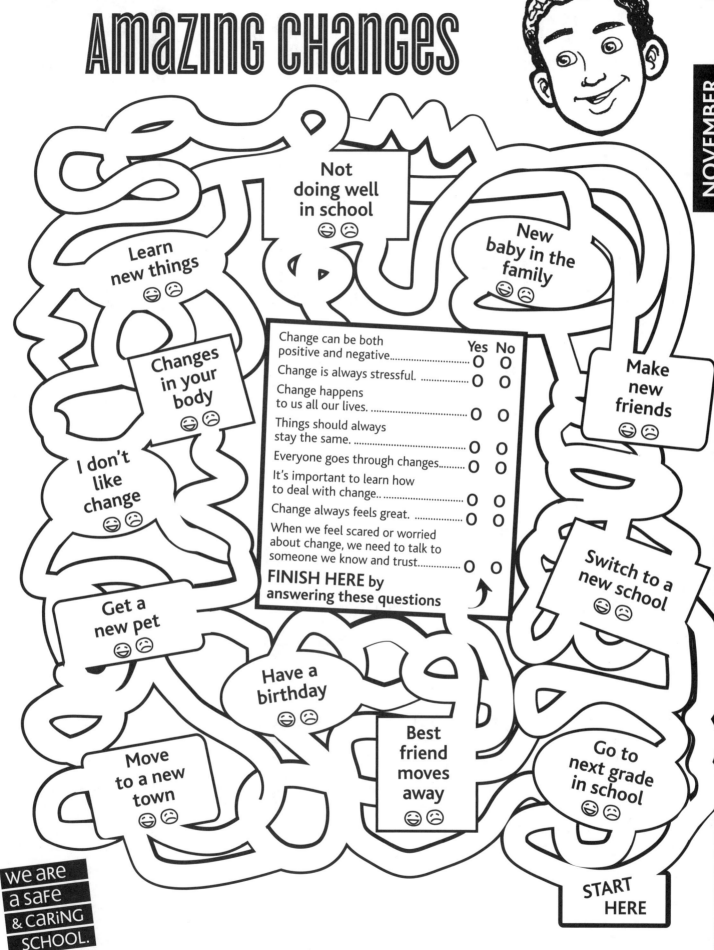

Not doing well in school 😄😞

Learn new things 😄😞

New baby in the family 😄😞

Changes in your body 😄😞

Make new friends 😄😞

I don't like change 😄😞

Change can be both positive and negative............................	Yes O	No O
Change is always stressful.	O	O
Change happens to us all our lives.	O	O
Things should always stay the same.	O	O
Everyone goes through changes..........	O	O
It's important to learn how to deal with change..	O	O
Change always feels great.	O	O
When we feel scared or worried about change, we need to talk to someone we know and trust................	O	O

FINISH HERE by answering these questions

Switch to a new school 😄😞

Get a new pet 😄😞

Have a birthday 😄😞

Best friend moves away 😄😞

Go to next grade in school 😄😞

Move to a new town 😄😞

START HERE

WHAT IS A FRIEND?

 NOVEMBER

What is **friendship**? _____

_____

_____

Why is it important to have friends? _____

_____

_____

What do you look for in a friend? _____

_____

_____

How do you make new friends? _____

_____

_____

How might a good friend get you in trouble? _____

_____

_____

we ARe
a SAFe
& CARiNG
SCHOOL.

RECIPE FOR A FRIEND

Pick your favorite ingredients!

	Yes	No
Caring	O	O
Doesn't share	O	O
Supportive	O	O
Bossy	O	O
Fun	O	O
Loud	O	O
Good listener	O	O
Smart	O	O
Teases people	O	O

	Yes	No
Spreads rumors	O	O
Trustworthy	O	O
Responsible	O	O

	Yes	No
Respectful	O	O
Kind	O	O
Likes school	O	O
Pushy	O	O
Know-it-all	O	O

	Yes	No
Dependable	O	O
Silly	O	O
Funny	O	O
Forgetful	O	O
Creative	O	O
Generous	O	O
Other?		
_____	O	O
_____	O	O

Friendship FLAVOR PACKET

Me

My Friend

What can you do to show you are a good friend?

_____

_____

_____

_____

_____

_____

we are a safe & caring school.

GIVE & TAKE

We need others, and others need us. Positive relationships are based on give and take.

People I ask for help	What I ask for	What can I do in return?
Mom	a ride to school	work harder to get good grades

Fill in the faces and words on this do-it-yourself cartoon to show a friend coming to you for help.

Friend   **You**   **Friend**   **You**

we are a safe & caring school.

GIFT FROM THE HEART

To:

From:

I care about you because...

STRESSING THE POSITIVE

Stress is part of life. Circle how stressful a situation can be on a scale from 1 to 4.

Choose two of your worst stressors. Write positive (+) and negative (−) ways you might handle them in the future.

Stress-O-Meter

	That's easy!	Interesting challenge	Why me?	Oh no!
doing homework	1	2	3	4
making friends	1	2	3	4
working on chores	1	2	3	4
talking to parents	1	2	3	4
the way I look	1	2	3	4
making choices	1	2	3	4
being on time	1	2	3	4
doing things right	1	2	3	4
someone is mad at me	1	2	3	4
being included	1	2	3	4
being liked	1	2	3	4
being responsible	1	2	3	4
being put on the spot	1	2	3	4
getting good grades	1	2	3	4

1)

2)

+ −   + −

we are a safe & caring school.

THEY MADE ME DO IT!

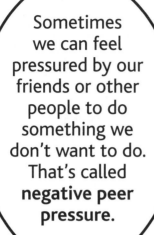

Can a friend get us in trouble? **Yes No** Explain.

_____

_____

Sometimes we can feel pressured by our friends or other people to do something we don't want to do. That's called **negative peer pressure.**

Did you ever go along with something other people did even though you knew it wasn't right? **Yes No** What happened?

_____

_____

_____

How did you feel? _____

_____

_____

Peer pressure can be positive or negative. Give examples of each.

What will you do next time? _____

_____

_____

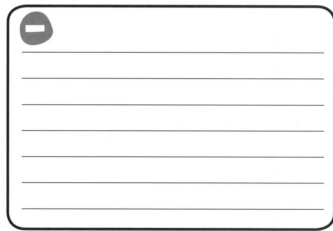

Draw a cartoon in the boxes below about a time when you experienced positive or negative peer preessure. How did you feel? What did you do?

we aRe a SaFe & CaRiNG SCHOOL.

CARING ABOUT COMPASSION

Another word for caring is compassion.

Write as many synonyms for compassion as you can fit in this caring heart.

Compassion means...

What happens when there is compassion at your safe and caring school?

Give an example of compassion you have seen.

What is the opposite of compassion?

What happens when there is no compassion?

Give an example from the news when compassion would have been helpful.

Research a historical figure known for compassion and answer these questions.

Who is the person and what did he or she do?	Where and when did this person live?	What did you learn about compassion from the person?

WE ARE A SAFE & CARING SCHOOL.

GETTING HELP & HELPING OTHERS

Define **empathy**.

_____
_____
_____
_____
_____

Caring how others feel is an important part of creating a safe and caring school.

What does empathy...

...look like?

...sound like?

...feel like?

Think of eight words that describe the skills we need to show empathy. Use as many of them as you can in a paragraph about helping others.

Empathy

we ARe a SaFe & CaRiNG SCHOOL.

MY SUPPORT SYSTEM QUIZ

True or False (circle the correct answer)

1) When things change in our lives, it can be stressful . . . . **True / False**

2) Change can be both positive and negative . . . . **True / False**

3) Tough people don't need anybody when they are feeling tired or stressed-out . . . . **True / False**

4) When we have empathy, we try to help others when they need support . . . . **True / False**

5) It is important to have people we can count on . . . . **True / False**

Multiple Choice (circle the correct answer)

6) At a Safe & Caring School:

   a. we support each other and care.

   b. we learn to give and ask for help.

   c. we make new friends and get along.

   d. all of the above.

7) Peer pressure is when:

   a. you go along with what others do even if you know it is wrong.

   b. your eyes are tired.

   c. the whole group encourages each other to follow the rules.

   d. a and c above.

8) We can tell how someone is feeling by:

   a. playing catch or jumping rope.

   b. listening carefully to the sound of his or her voice.

   c. watching his ir her face and body language.

   d. b and c above.

Fill in the Blanks

9) Another word for caring is **c**_____.

10) Stress can be **p**_____or **n**_____.

Real-Life Writing

Friends help each other stay out of trouble. What would you say to a friend who wants you to do something you know might be fun, but is against the rules?

From *Safe & Caring Schools® Grades 3–5* by Katia S. Petersen, Ph.D., copyright © 2008. Free Spirit Publishing Inc., Minneapolis, MN; www.freespirit.com. This page may be photocopied for individual, classroom, or small group work only. For other uses, call 800-735-7323.

Safe & Caring Schools®

SKILLS FOR SCHOOL. SKILLS FOR LIFE.

DECEMBER
Respect Yourself and Others

- **Community**
- **Respect**
- **Manners**
- **Communication Skills**
- **Helping Others**
- **Inclusion**

Belonging to a community means getting along with others, having a special place, and knowing what others expect of you. It is important for children to understand that as active participants of their school community they help create a safe and caring environment. The more we teach children to get along, the more responsible and productive they will become.

MONTHLY OBJECTIVES
Students will:

- learn specific ways they can be responsible members of their school community
- practice using good manners to show respect

TEACHING TIPS

- Teaching the golden rule is a priority in a safe and caring environment. We must help kids understand that respect is a mutual character trait.
- Empathy is the ability to understand, predict, and relate to someone's feelings. Without empathy, children will have a difficult time resolving problems in peaceful ways. If we cultivate empathy while our children are young, it becomes natural for them.
- Model empathy and the golden rule as often as you can.

DECEMBER INTEGRATED ACTIVITIES

In addition to the specific lesson plans for this month, you can use these optional ideas to integrate and extend the Safe & Caring themes into your daily routines and across curricular areas.

LANGUAGE ARTS

- Have students write stories about good manners, appreciation, and equality.
- Create a classroom book with short stories and pictures about inclusion.
- Organize a special "Author's Day" for students to read their works to parents and other special guests.
- Read "The Visitor," a poem by Jack Prelutsky, to the class. It uses humor to look at not-so-nice behaviors. Have students rewrite the poem by changing the disrespectful behaviors into good behaviors.
- Read "Manners," a poem by Elizabeth Bishop. Compare and contrast the manners of 1918 to the manners of today.

LITERATURE

- Visit your school or public library to have students read books about great citizens of their country (for example: Susan B. Anthony, Elizabeth Blackwell, Ben Franklin, Eleanor Roosevelt, Cesar Chavez, Martin Luther King, Jr., Rosa Parks, Frederick Douglass, Jane Addams, or Roger Williams). Have students prepare and present short biographies to the class.
- If you have an established book review day, ask each student or a small group of students to find a creative way to present book reviews to the class.
- Read books about respect and equality like *The Paper Bag Princess* by Robert N. Munsch, or *Prince Cinders* by Babette Cole.

SOCIAL STUDIES

- Have students observe and record how other children treat the school and its property. Do they see positive, respectful behaviors or negative, disrespectful behaviors? Brainstorm what they can do to enhance or change those behaviors.
- Take a walk around the school community. Discuss the history of the neighborhood and the school. Explain to students that an important part of good citizenship is having a sense of pride in their community.
- Celebrate Human Rights Day on December 10 by discussing how respect, manners, helping others, and inclusion relate to human rights issues. Read *Kids Around the World Celebrate! The Best Feasts and Festivals from Many Lands* by Lynda Jones.

ART

- Have students design a school bulletin board describing what it means to be respectful.
- Talk about graffiti. Show students examples of it. Ask: What is it? Why do people do it? Is it respectful of other people's property? Can graffiti be used in a positive way?
- Create posters or murals to show ways students and adults can make everyone feel part of their school community.
- Create posters that show how good manners can contribute to spreading peace within the school.

MUSIC

- Work with students to write a song or rap about respect, honesty, or being part of a community. For inspiration and ideas listen to *Ready to Rock Kids*, Volumes 1 & 2, by Dr. Mac & Friends.

MATH

- Have students design puzzles using geometric shapes or tessellations. Write one of the Safe & Caring vocabulary words on each puzzle piece before students cut them out. Distribute the pieces randomly to the class. Work cooperatively to put the puzzle together.
- Celebrate Crossword Puzzle Day on December 21 by creating puzzles about respect that students can share with other classes.

Safe & Caring Vocabulary and Word Find

LEARNING OBJECTIVES

Students will:

- be introduced to vocabulary that supports respecting yourself and others
- internalize the vocabulary as they use it throughout the month and year in real-life situations

MATERIALS NEEDED

"Safe & Caring Vocabulary" (page 82) and "Safe & Caring Word Find" (page 83) activity sheets, pencils, dictionaries

LESSON PLAN

Use the vocabulary activities to introduce the concepts and common language associated with this month's theme. Throughout the month, use the words in writing, spelling, storytelling, and dealing with conflict situations.

For "Safe & Caring Schools Vocabulary," explain how to use the secret code to decipher the message. (*Manners* involve both the *words* and *actions* we use. When we speak *politely*, it helps everyone get along. When we are *rude*, it is hard to build *friendships*. *Put-downs* and *blaming* can cause *conflict*, but being *honest* and giving an *apology* shows others we want to be part of a *respectful* school community.)

For "Safe & Caring Word Find," discuss what the words mean after completing the page. You may want students to work in pairs to help each other.

Compliment Calendar

LEARNING OBJECTIVES

Students will:

- identify what put-downs are and learn how to choose alternate words
- learn what compliments are and practice using respectful words and actions

MATERIALS NEEDED

The book *Princess Penelope's Parrot* by Helen Lester, "Compliment Calendar" activity sheet (page 84), "Thumbs-Up Tokens" (page 85), writing tools

LESSON PLAN

READ *Princess Penelope's Parrot*. Spoiled Princess Penelope cannot get her new parrot to talk, so she threatens it and calls it nasty names. But when Prince Percival comes courting, the parrot gets revenge on the greedy princess in a hilarious way.

DISCUSS how Princess Penelope treated her parrot. Why do you think the parrot decided not to talk? What lesson did Princess Penelope learn about choosing to use unkind words? Have students create a list of situations where people use put-downs to get their way. Using the list, have students role-play the difference between put-downs and compliments. Review I-messages and Stop, Think, Choose skills.

As an option, have students create short skits showing respectful ways to deal with problems. (Review skits prior to sharing with the class to ensure appropriate language and solutions to each problem.)

DO the "Compliment Calendar" activity sheet. Copy and cut out the "Thumbs-Up Tokens" from the template for use on the calendars. At the end of each day, give the students who used respectful words and actions a "Thumbs-Up" to glue to their calendars.

RELATE the activity to classroom life by reminding students that put-downs hurt people's feelings. This is a good opportunity to review the concept of consequences.

Time for Respect

LEARNING OBJECTIVES

Students will:

- gain a better understanding of what respect means and how good manners contribute to it
- learn about respecting others' feelings, ideas, and beliefs.

MATERIALS NEEDED

The book *Crow Boy* by Taro Yashima, "Time for Respect" activity sheet (page 86), writing and drawing tools

LESSON PLAN

READ   *Crow Boy*. Students try to understand the behavior of a new kid in their class, and they develop an awareness for individual differences.

> As an option for independent reading or teacher modeled and shared reading use *The Crying Christmas Tree* by Allan Crow. When a grandmother is upset with her grandchildren's lack of sensitivity, she is consoled with the thought that her grandchildren will eventually learn that respect and understanding are important ingredients in life. This is an Ojibwe tale.

DISCUSS   the meaning of the golden rule. Explain to children that when they use good manners, they are choosing to treat others with respect. Ask children to give you examples of how people show respect for each other. *(Examples may include paying attention when someone is speaking, not interrupting, not pushing, and using kind words.)*

DO   the "Time for Respect" activity sheet. Children work in small groups to draw pictures or write short stories about how they can show respect and how others have shown respect to them.

RELATE   the pictures and stories shared by students to school life. Remind students that demonstrating good manners means using kind words and actions to show respect at school, at home, and in their communities.

A Better Way to Say It

LEARNING OBJECTIVES

Students will:

- learn that safe and caring words need to be part of their vocabulary
- gain a better understanding that their words and actions affect other people in positive or negative ways

MATERIALS NEEDED

The book *Manners* by Aliki, "A Better Way to Say It" activity sheet (page 87), writing and drawing tools

LESSON PLAN

READ   *Manners*. This book introduces manners as polite and accepted ways to treat others with respect.

DISCUSS   the concepts from the book and practice new vocabulary words. Help children understand they can choose to use respectful words and actions to help them get along with others. Tell students that choosing to be rude and unkind hurts people's feelings and makes it harder to keep friends.

DO   the "A Better Way to Say It" activity sheet. Ask children to rewrite unkind sayings with positive words.

RELATE   Review respectful words and actions students can use every day. This will help them understand that they play a part in creating and maintaining a safe and caring classroom and school environment.

Lining Up Good Manners

LEARNING OBJECTIVES

Students will:

- review the difference between good and bad manners
- practice using good manners

MATERIALS NEEDED

The book *Mrs. Peloki's Substitute* by Joanne Oppenheim, "Lining Up Good Manners" activity sheet (page 88), writing and drawing tools, scissors, envelopes

LESSON PLAN

READ   *Mrs. Peloki's Substitute*. When a substitute teacher comes to Mrs. Peloki's classroom, everyone forgets to use good manners.

DISCUSS   what happens when people forget to use good manners. What are the consequences of using bad manners? Remind students how important it is to use good manners at all times, especially when they have visitors at their school or in the classroom.

DO   the "Lining Up Good Manners" activity sheet in small groups. Have students cut out the 24 squares and separate the good manners (11 squares) from the bad manners (13 squares). Then, using the boldfaced letter on each square, have students line up the squares to spell two words related to this lesson *(good manners)*.

RELATE   how important good manners are for getting along with others. Review examples of respectful and disrespectful behavior from the activity sheet. Do students understand how the language and concepts they are learning translate into the behavior expected of them in your classroom? Relate this activity to the Safe & Caring Promise, the Safe & Caring Rules, and the Golden Rule posters and activities.

My Story of Acceptance

LEARNING OBJECTIVES

Students will:

- learn to appreciate diversity
- understand that everyone deserves respect and equality

MATERIALS NEEDED

The book *Grandmama's Pride* by Becky Birtha, "Acceptance Acrostic Poem" activity sheet (page 89), writing and drawing tools

LESSON PLAN

READ   *Grandmama's Pride*. A 1956 visit to their grandmother's house in the South exposes two African-American girls to segregation and prejudice they never experienced in the North.

> Optional reading for independent reading time or teacher modeled and shared reading could include *Felita* by Nicholasa Mohr. Felita moves to a new neighborhood, and her neighbors taunt her family because they are from Puerto Rico.

DISCUSS   What was different between the girls' experience on the bus and at the bus station? How did things change? What was Grandmama's pride, and why was it too big to sit in the back of the bus? What did the girls learn about segregation and prejudice? Why is it hard for some people to accept others?

DO   the "Acceptance Acrostic Poem" activity sheet. Students work individually to create a poem using the letters of the word *acceptance* as the first letter in a sentence about or describing acceptance.

RELATE   the concept of acceptance to the kids' lives by sharing the poems they wrote. Discuss ways students can show acceptance at school and home every day. Display the poems around the school, or create a classroom book titled, "We Accept Each Other."

I'm Not to Blame

LEARNING OBJECTIVES

Students will:

- learn the importance of being responsible for their actions
- explore what to do when blamed unfairly

MATERIALS NEEDED

The book *Arthur and the True Francine* by Marc Brown, "I Am Not to Blame!" activity sheet (page 90), writing and drawing tools

LESSON PLAN

READ   *Arthur and the True Francine*. Francine and Muffy are good friends until Muffy lets Francine take the blame for cheating on a test.

DISCUSS   What does it mean to be responsible for your own actions? Help students realize that their actions are a result of their choices.

DO   the "I Am Not to Blame!" activity sheet. Students complete it by drawing pictures and writing captions to create a cartoon story about blaming.

RELATE   the lesson to real-life situations by sharing the cartoon stories during class. Review the concept of being responsible for your own actions. Discuss how easy it is to misunderstand the words or actions of other people. Remind students to ask questions to clarify a situation before they say or do something hurtful.

My Apologies

LEARNING OBJECTIVES

Students will:

- define *apology* and discuss when apologies are necessary
- explore personal responsibility and learn how to improve relationships by using apologies

MATERIALS NEEDED

The book *Sorry!* by Trudy Ludwig, "My Apologies" activity sheet (page 91), writing tools

LESSON PLAN

READ   *Sorry!* When Jack's friend Charlie ruins Leena's science project, an insincere "sorry" just won't cut it. Jack learns the importance of an apology.

DISCUSS   why it is important to apologize. How does one go about it? Students have the right to feel upset when someone treats them disrespectfully. Talk about how apologizing is not an easy thing to do, especially when students feel very angry. How important is it to take time to calm down before attempting an apology and forgiveness.

DO   the "My Apologies" activity sheet. Ask students to write a short story about a time they needed to apologize to someone or a time they deserved an apology. Students may draw pictures to illustrate their stories.

RELATE   how important it is to apologize when we do something wrong. Ask for volunteers to share their short stories. Review the three steps of how to apologize: 1) Look at the person; 2) Say it like you mean it; 3) Use respectful words. Emphasize that it takes courage to apologize and forgive.

Let's Be Honest

LEARNING OBJECTIVES

Students will:

- explore the meaning of *honesty*
- discuss the consequences of not being honest

MATERIALS NEEDED

The book *The Empty Pot* by Demi, "Let's Be Honest" activity sheet (page 92), writing and drawing tools

LESSON PLAN

READ   *The Empty Pot.* A young boy with a green thumb wins the emperor's competition because he chooses to tell the truth.

> An optional book for independent reading or teacher modeled and shared reading is *Liar, Liar, Pants on Fire* by Gordon Korman. Zoe's lies lead to telling more lies to cover the ones she told before. As a result, no one believes her, even when she tells the truth.

DISCUSS   What is the definition of *honesty?* Why do you think it is important to be honest? What was the emperor really looking for in the story? How did he find it?

DO   the "Let's Be Honest" activity sheet. Each student draws a picture and writes an explanation of what honesty looks like in a safe and caring school.

RELATE   the activity to daily life by asking students to share their drawings with the class. Collect the pictures and create a classroom display about honesty.

Equality and Stereotypes

LEARNING OBJECTIVES

Students will:

- define and understand the meaning of *stereotypes*
- review the positive and negative effects of stereotyping

MATERIALS NEEDED

The book *Trading Places with Tank Talbott* by Dori Hillestad Butler, "Equality and Stereotypes" activity sheet (page 93), writing tools

LESSON PLAN

READ   *Trading Places with Tank Talbott.* Jason is miserable. He's being forced by his parents to learn how to swim. To make matters worse, a staff person at the recreation center mistakes him for Tank, the neighborhood bully who looks just like him.

DISCUSS Why is Jason so miserable and upset? What is Tank's favorite thing to do? How did Jason and Tank end up trading places? After they switch places, how are they treated? Why? Is stereotyping a good thing or a bad thing? Why? Are all people treated equally? If not, why not? Why do people choose to stereotype? Have you ever felt that you were treated differently because of who you are? What did you do about it?

DO the "Equality and Stereotypes" activity sheet.

RELATE the lesson to the students' personal lives by reviewing the completed activity sheets and asking students to define *stereotypes* and *equality*. Have students give examples of each.

Nobody Left Out

LEARNING OBJECTIVES

Students will:

- define discrimination and discover its relationship to stereotyping
- identify ways people are excluded and determine how they can promote inclusion

MATERIALS NEEDED

The book *A Day's Work* by Eve Bunting, "Nobody Left Out" activity sheet (page 94), writing tools

LESSON PLAN

READ *A Day's Work*. Francisco helps his grandfather find work as a gardener even though his grandfather knows nothing about gardening. When his employer finds out, Francisco has to make things right.

DISCUSS How was Francisco trying to help his grandfather? Was he honest about what his grandfather could do? How did the employer feel about the situation? What did Francisco do to make things right? What is the definition of *discrimination*. How is stereotyping related to discrimination? What can people do to prevent stereotyping?

DO the "Nobody Left Out" activity sheet. Ask students to write about times they have seen others excluded and ways they can help include others.

RELATE the lesson to real-life situations. Review completed activity sheets. What did the class record as ways students are excluded? What can the class do to correct those exclusions?

Respect Yourself and Others Quiz

To assess student progress, use the quiz on page 95. *(Answers: 1- F, 2-T, 3-F, 4-T, 5-F, 6-a, 7-d, 8-d, 9-manners, respect, 10-accept)*

Safe & Caring Vocabulary

Use the code to spell the missing words.

a	b	c	d	e	f	g	h	i	j	k	l	m	n	o	p	q	r	s	t	u	v	w	x	y	z

_ _ _ _ _ _ _ involve both the _ _ _ _ _ and

_ _ _ _ _ _ _ _ we use. When we speak _ _ _ _ _ _ _ _ _,

it helps everyone get along. When we are

_ _ _ _, it is hard to build _ _ _ _ _ _ _ _ _ _ _.

_ _ _ – _ _ _ _ _ and _ _ _ _ _ _ _ _ can cause

_ _ _ _ _ _ _ _ _, but being _ _ _ _ _ _ and giving

an _ _ _ _ _ _ _ shows others we want to be

part of a _ _ _ _ _ _ _ _ _ _ _ school community.

Define the word **respect**. _____

_____

_____

What is the opposite of respect? _____ Why does it
not belong in a safe and caring school? _____

_____

we are
a safe
& caring
school.

SAFE & CARING WORD FIND

Find and circle the words listed at the bottom of the page.

(Hint: Answers can run forward, backward, up, down, or diagonally.)

C	O	N	S	E	Q	U	E	N	C	E	F
A	C	T	I	O	N	S	O	S	S	A	O
R	A	L	P	H	C	P	F	U	S	P	R
D	I	V	E	R	S	I	T	Y	N	O	G
I	N	G	R	M	I	A	N	L	W	L	I
S	C	O	B	L	A	M	E	Y	O	O	V
R	L	L	D	U	J	E	V	I	D	G	E
E	U	D	E	Q	U	A	L	I	T	Y	N
S	S	E	M	E	D	G	C	R	U	D	E
P	I	N	A	T	G	X	V	E	P	E	S
E	O	R	N	I	E	V	M	S	S	R	S
C	N	U	R	W	O	B	A	P	O	A	F
T	O	L	I	O	H	O	N	E	S	T	Y
F	S	E	N	R	O	Y	N	C	R	E	C
U	O	S	Y	D	B	S	E	T	Z	I	M
L	J	L	O	S	A	T	R	F	F	I	S
S	K	I	N	S	N	E	S	U	L	A	Q
O	S	S	E	N	E	T	I	L	O	P	P

WORDS	INCLUSION	RUDE	APOLOGY
ACTIONS	MANNERS	JUDGE	GOLDEN RULE
PUT-DOWNS	HONESTY	DISRESPECTFUL	
BLAME	FORGIVENESS	CONSEQUENCE	
RESPECTFUL	POLITENESS	GIRLS	
DIVERSITY	EQUALITY	BOYS	

we are
a safe
& caring
SCHOOL.

DECEMBER

COMPLIMENT CALENDAR

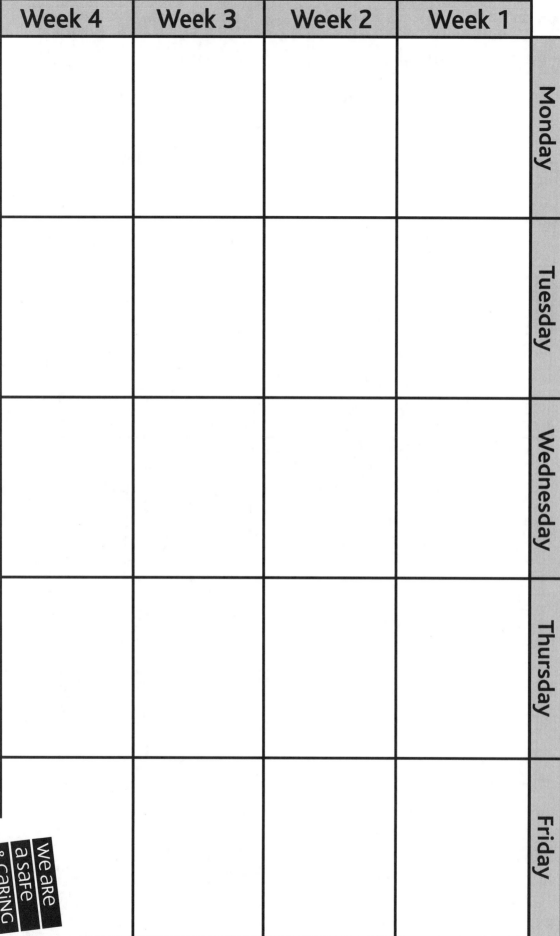

	Week 4	Week 3	Week 2	Week 1
Monday				
Tuesday				
Wednesday				
Thursday				
Friday				

WE ARE
A SAFE
& CARING
SCHOOL.

THUMBS UP TOKENS

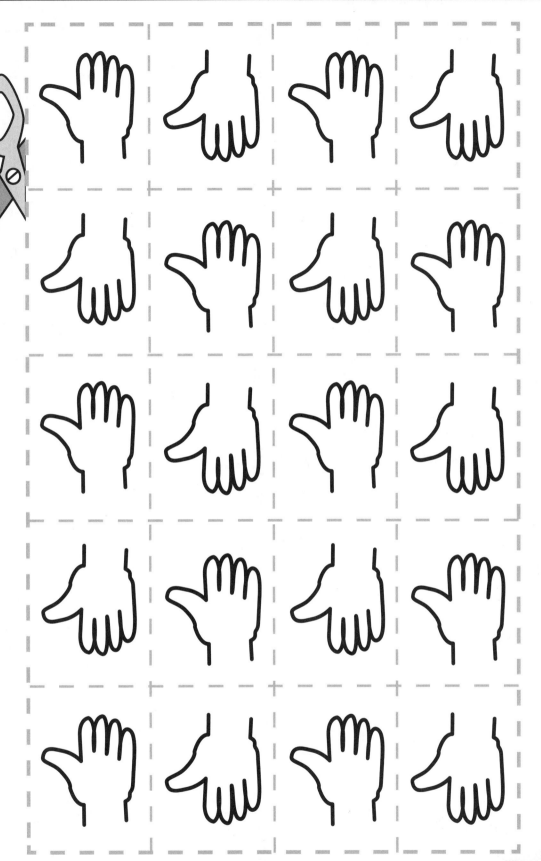

TIME FOR RESPECT

A time I showed respect to someone

What happened

How I felt

What I chose to do

A time someone showed respect to me

What happened

How I felt

What I chose to do

We are a safe & caring school.

A BETTER WAY TO SAY IT

Disrespectful	Respectful
Go away, and leave me alone!	
Give me the remote control now! It's my favorite show!	
Don't you dare touch my things!	
If you don't do what I want, I won't be your friend anymore.	
Your picture is so stupid. You are terrible at drawing.	
Other:	

we aRe
a SaFe
& CaRiNG
SCHOOL.

LINING UP GOOD MANNERS

Cleaning up **a**fter a project	Calling someone a **b**ad name when you're angry	Screaming when you **w**ant something	Helping with ch**o**res
Laughing at someone because of how he or she **l**ooks	Saying please and tha**n**k you	**P**ushing people	**T**hrowing things on the floor
Waiting for your tur**n**	**H**itting someone when you're angry	Shaking hands wh**e**n you meet someone	Grabbing food without as**k**ing
Interru**p**ting	Using kind w**o**rds	Talking with your mouth **f**ull	Sharin**g**
Using put-downs to be fun**n**y	Helping a frien**d**	Opening the doo**r** for someone	Not pa**y**ing attention
Helping clean up after a **m**eal	**C**utting in line	Saying "could you plea**s**e pass the…"	Telling disgusting **j**okes while you eat

we are
a safe
& caring
school.

ACCEPTANCE ACROSTIC POEM

It's important to respect and accept others in our community and include them in things we do.

A

C

C

E

P

T

A

N

C

E

we are a safe & caring school.

I AM NOT TO BLAME!

we are
a safe
& caring
SCHOOL.

MY APOLOGIES

Define the word **apology**. _____

_____

_____

Why is it important to apologize? _____

_____

_____

_____

_____

Write about a time when you needed
to apologize to someone. What happened?
How did you feel? What did you choose to do?

_____

_____

_____

_____

_____

_____

_____

_____

_____

_____

we are
a safe
& caring
school.

DECEMBER

LET'S BE HONEST

What does **honesty** look like?

How does honesty help us get along at our safe and caring school?

_____

_____

_____

_____

_____

_____

we aRe
a saFe
& CaRiNG
SCHOOL.

Equality and Stereotypes

In a safe & caring school we treat each other as equals.

1 Describe what **equal** means to you.

2 What are some things you can do to treat people equally?

Sometimes we think differently about people because of their culture or the way they look or sound.

3 Define **stereotype**.

4 List some stereotypes you might see in movies or read in books.

Have you ever been treated unfairly just because of who you are? What happened? _____

How did it make you feel? _____
What did you do about it? _____

We are a safe & caring school.

NOBODY LEFT OUT

Being left out is no fun at all. That's why we choose to include everyone at our safe and caring school.

What are some ways kids exclude others at school?

When we leave someone out, we **exclude** them.

Write three ways you can help someone who has been excluded in your classroom or school.

 1

 2

 3

we are a safe & caring school.

RESPECT YOURSELF AND OTHERS QUIZ

True or False (circle the correct answer)

1) Good manners are for little kids. When you get older you don't need to use them anymore . . . . **True / False**

2) Compliments are nice to get, but also great to give to others. . . . . **True / False**

3) The best way to get respect is by making sure people know you're better than they are. . . . . **True / False**

4) Everyone makes mistakes. When we apologize we show others that we respect them. . . . . . . **True / False**

5) Being honest is for losers. Winners do whatever it takes to win . . . . **True / False**

Multiple Choice (circle the correct answer)

6) At a Safe & Caring School:
   - **a.** we treat each other as equals.
   - **b.** we use stereotypes so we know how to treat each other.
   - **c.** girls and boys don't need to get along.
   - **d.** all of the above.

7) Inclusion means:
   - **a.** nobody gets left out.
   - **b.** everybody has a chance to learn, grow, and have fun.
   - **c.** all students are part of the school community.
   - **d.** all of the above.

8) Examples of bad manners in class would be:
   - **a.** not paying attention.
   - **b.** interrupting.
   - **c.** waiting for your turn.
   - **d.** a and b above.

Fill in the Blanks

9) Good **m**_____ show **r**_____.

10) When we respect others, we **a**_____ them for who they are.

Real-Life Writing

How do we make everyone feel welcome and accepted at our Safe & Caring School?

we are a safe & caring school.

JANUARY
Bullying

- **Empathy**
- **Bullying**
- **Teasing**

In a world where conflict, violence, drugs, and weapons have a daily presence, the ability to empathize is vital. Children who lack the skills of empathy and compassion may have difficulty with impulse control, which can lead to conflict. The wrong look, a side comment, or an accidental push can quickly escalate into a major confrontation. With the appropriate skills, the magnitude of conflicts can be reduced. Our children will learn to care if we make time to model empathy.

MONTHLY OBJECTIVES
Students will:

- learn to understand and accept people because of what they have on the inside
- practice empathy skills as they learn the importance of compassion and kindness

TEACHING TIPS

- In daily interaction with students, we often say, "Yes, I am listening," yet children complain that we do not really hear what they are trying to tell us. We need to listen not only with our ears but also with our hearts. When we listen with our hearts, we are better able to understand the subtle yet important messages children are trying to give us.

- We want to be proactive and anticipate potential conflict in order to prevent disruptions in teaching and learning.

In addition to the specific lesson plans for this month, you can use these optional ideas to integrate and extend the Safe & Caring themes into your daily routines and across curricular areas.

LANGUAGE ARTS

- Have students define and discuss the word *caring*. What are synonyms and antonyms of *caring?* Is it a noun, verb, adverb, or adjective?

- Create a "Classroom of Kindness" book. Students can record whenever they see kindness to others or when others show kindness to them. Share the completed book during circle time at the end of the week.

- Divide students into small groups. Ask each group to come up with a list of words and actions that describe kindness, compassion, and acceptance. Use the list to write short stories showing how these skills help us get along with others.

- Ask students to write in journals about a time they have experienced bullying. Give students the option to share their journal entries with the class.

LITERATURE

- Read *Martin's Big Words: The Life of Martin Luther King, Jr.* by Doreen Rappaport. Have students identify times when Dr. King showed compassion, equality, acceptance, and kindness.

- Read real-life stories about young people who are everyday heroes. Explain that a hero is someone who is kind, helpful, and brave. Tell the students about the everyday heroes in your life (including them!).

- Discuss community, national, or world leaders who have worked for equal rights for all people. Have students identify common characteristics among these leaders.

- Read books about teasing and bullying behaviors. (for example: *Just Kidding* by Trudy Ludwig or *A Bad Case of Tattle Tongue* by Julia Cook). Have students write their own stories about bullying, teasing, and tattling.

ART

- Use a camera to take pictures of students as they role-play the right and wrong ways to deal with bullies. Post the pictures with captions, or create a classroom book about bullies.

- Using "No Bullying Allowed in Our School" as a theme, students can decorate bulletin boards in the hallways, the cafeteria, or entryway of your school.

- Help students make kindness cards to give to people who have been kind to them. See the "Gift from the Heart" template (page 69).

- Have students create miniposters showing the meaning of empathy.

MUSIC

- Teach songs related to the struggles for equal rights, such as "We Shall Overcome," "Blowin' in the Wind," or "This Little Light of Mine." Have students identify how lyrics and melody help express the emotions of the time.

MATH

- Ask students to create a chart that shows how many acts of kindness they witnessed during the month. To make it more interesting, have each classroom in a grade level keep its own chart, and compare the charts at the end of the month. Recognize all attempts to use acts of kindness.

- Students write word problems related to the monthly theme. (For example, Mary helped her mother with the dishes for 7 days, walked her elderly neighbor's dog for 6 days, and read a book to her sister for 5 nights. How many acts of kindness did Mary do? If Mary did this every month for a year, how many acts of kindness would that be?) Kids write their own word problems using names of their classmates. Write the problems on index cards, and pass them out for others to solve.

Safe & Caring Vocabulary and Word Find

LEARNING OBJECTIVES

Students will:

- be introduced to vocabulary that supports caring about others and preventing bullying behaviors
- internalize the vocabulary as they use it throughout the month and year in real-life situations

MATERIALS NEEDED

"Safe & Caring Vocabulary" (page 103) and "Safe and Caring Word Find" (page 104), dictionaries, pencils

LESSON PLAN

Use the vocabulary activities to introduce the concepts and common language associated with this month's theme. Throughout the month, use the words in writing, spelling, storytelling, and dealing with conflict situations.

For "Safe & Caring Schools Vocabulary," explain how to unscramble the words to complete the paragraph and decipher the message. (Sometimes people _choose_ to get what they want by being _bullies_, but _name-calling_, _teasing_, and _violence_ are not the _safe_ and _caring_ school's way. We can stop bullying when we take the time to _understand_ how someone else _feels_. When we try to see things from the other person's _view_, we learn to have _empathy_ for them and make _positive_ choices to help us _get along_.)

For "Safe & Caring Word Find," discuss what the words mean after completing the page. You may want students to work in pairs to help each other.

Too Quick to Judge

LEARNING OBJECTIVES

Students will:

- understand the importance of getting to know people on the inside instead of judging them from the outside
- learn that bullying is a learned behavior that they can work to change

MATERIALS NEEDED

The book _Enemy Pie_ by Derek Munson, a brown paper lunch bag (one per student), construction paper, writing and drawing tools, scissors, glue

LESSON PLAN

READ   _Enemy Pie_. It is a perfect summer until Jeremy Ross moves into the house down the street and becomes neighborhood enemy number one. Luckily, Dad has a surefire way to get rid of enemies: Enemy Pie. But, part of the secret recipe is spending an entire day playing with the enemy!

An optional text for independent reading or teacher modeled and shared reading is _The Bully of Barkham Street_ by Mary Stolz. Feeling misunderstood at home and at school, Martin Hastings becomes a bully. When he finds he has no friends and a bad reputation, Martin decides to make a change.

DISCUSS   what the students learned from the story about understanding and accepting others. Everyone wants to feel included in a group, so ask the students what they can do to help everyone feel included.

_DO_   Ask students to draw pictures or write about the things that describe themselves (for example, their favorite books, things they enjoy doing after school, their talents, how many people in their families). Have students place their drawings or stories inside their bags. The outside of the bag represents the way the students look on the outside. Using construction paper or other art supplies, have students create an image of themselves on the outside of the bag.

RELATE   the lesson to daily life by having students share things about their inside and outside selves. Remind students that we are more alike than different and understanding this helps us get along.

The Problem with Bullying

LEARNING OBJECTIVES

Students will:

- explore the meaning of bullying behaviors and reflect upon their own experiences with bullying
- learn practical strategies to help them deal with bullying in nonviolent ways, including how to be a positive bystander

MATERIALS NEEDED

The book *My Secret Bully* by Trudy Ludwig, "The Problem with Bullying" activity sheet (page 105), writing and drawing tools

LESSON PLAN

READ   *My Secret Bully*. Two girls have been friends since kindergarten, but lately one excludes and embarrasses the other in front of their classmates.

DISCUSS   the bullying behaviors in the story *(pushing, yelling, and more)*. Help students identify how the characters felt while they were being bullied. Ask: What was the problem between Monica and Katie? How did Monica feel about the way Katie treated her? To whom did she reach out for help? How did Monica solve the problem? What does bullying look like, and why do people bully? What types of bullying have you seen? Review specific things students can do when they encounter bullies *(stay calm, use I-messages, say "stop," don't fight, tell an adult)*.

DO   "The Problem with Bullying" activity sheet, having students write from their own experiences.

RELATE   the lesson to the students' lives by asking volunteers to share their work on the activity sheets. Discuss positive options for dealing with kids who bully. Tell students that although they are learning new skills to deal with bullying, they will not always be able to solve problems alone. Encourage them to ask for help from someone they know and trust.

Mean Words Hurt

LEARNING OBJECTIVES

Students will:

- review how words can hurt just as much as actions
- practice dealing with difficult situations with positive communication

MATERIALS NEEDED

The book *But Names Will Never Hurt Me* by Bernard Waber, "Mean Words Hurt" activity sheet (page 106), writing and drawing tools

LESSON PLAN

READ   *But Names Will Never Hurt Me*. Alison Wonderland is teased by others because of her name. She finds a positive way to resolve the problem.

DISCUSS   why students choose to tease. Why was Alison teased? How did she feel about it? What can friends do to help each other when one is being teased?

DO   the "Mean Words Hurt" activity sheet. Students complete the sheet by evaluating what is happening in each scenario.

RELATE   the lesson to real life by asking students to share their work with classmates. Allow children to discuss their thoughts about hurtful words. When do they hear them the most? What can they do about it?

A Kid's View on Bullies

LEARNING OBJECTIVES

Students will:

- review and discuss how to cope with bullying behavior
- create a personal journal sheet to explore bullying

MATERIALS NEEDED

The book: *Stop Picking on Me* by Pat Thomas, "A Kid's View on Bullies" activity sheet. (page 107), writing tools

LESSON PLAN

READ   *Stop Picking on Me*. This picture book explores the issue of bullying among children. It helps kids accept the normal fears and worries that accompany bullying and suggests ways to handle the problem.

> An option for independent reading or teacher modeled and shared reading is *Bullies Are a Pain in the Brain* by Trevor Romain. This book blends humor with serious, practical suggestions for coping with bullying behavior.

DISCUSS   what the class learned today about bullying and how to deal with it.

DO the activity sheet, having each student work independently to thoughtfully answer the questions. Be sensitive to answers related to bullies in families and among friends.

RELATE the issue of bullying to school life by reviewing the students' completed sheets. Develop an action plan to help students bring the issue of bullying into the open. How can they be positive bystanders to support one another when confronted with bullying?

Helping Our Friends Stop Bullying

LEARNING OBJECTIVES

Students will:

- learn about positive and negative bystanders
- explore ways they can be positive bystanders and develop support systems

MATERIALS NEEDED

The book *Nobody Knew What to Do: A Story About Bullying* by Becky Ray McCain, "Helping Our Friends Stop Bullying" activity sheet (page 108), writing tools

LESSON PLAN

READ *Nobody Knew What to Do: A Story About Bullying.* When a boy at school is bullied by other kids, a classmate decides that he must do something, even if he is a bit afraid.

DISCUSS what happened to Ray. Why were kids picking on him? How did some of the students help Ray stand up to the bullies?

DO the "Helping Our Friends Stop Bullying" activity sheet. Direct students to write responses to the different bullying situations.

RELATE the activity to student life by discussing ways to help kids who are being bullied. Ask: Why do students choose to stand and watch but not to get involved in a bullying situation? What can we do to help stop bullying at school? Discuss being a positive bystander.

The Other Person's Shoes

LEARNING OBJECTIVES

Students will:

- review the concept of empathy
- learn what they can do to support others who need help

MATERIALS NEEDED

The book *Say Something* by Peggy Moss, "The Other Person's Shoes" activity sheet (page 109), writing and drawing tools

LESSON PLAN

READ *Say Something.* After watching other kids bully and tease the kids, a young girl realizes she can no longer stand and watch as others get hurt.

DISCUSS Explain to students that it is sometimes hard to know what to do when we see a friend in trouble. Review how the girl in the story empathized with her classmate, and how she got the courage to help. Brainstorm ideas about what the students can do to help stop bullying.

DO "The Other Person's Shoes" activity sheet. Have students think of an actual situation they know and then answer the questions.

RELATE Ask volunteers to share their answers on the activity sheet in order to talk about real situations and how the students can put themselves in the shoes of the person who needs their help. Then turn the situation around and ask what would happen if they put themselves in the shoes of the person who is bullying others.

Just Kidding

LEARNING OBJECTIVES

Students will:

- learn the difference between kidding and teasing and the effects they have on people
- review kidding or teasing situations and use a rating scale to determine the severity of each

MATERIALS NEEDED

The book *Just Kidding* by Trudy Ludwig, "Just Kidding!" activity sheet (page 110), writing tools

LESSON PLAN

READ *Just Kidding.* This is the story of a bully who uses words in hurtful ways, and then uses the excuse of "just kidding" to stay out of trouble.

DISCUSS What did Vince do to bully Cody? How did Cody feel, and what did he do when he was teased? Who helped Cody figure out what to do? Challenge students to articulate how they know when a comment is mean or offensive rather than funny. Record their answers on the board.

DO the "Just Kidding!" activity sheet. Ask students to write three ways they can recognize when kidding crosses the line and becomes hurtful teasing. Students will also rate situations as to whether or not they are kidding or teasing.

RELATE what students learned from the lesson to the classroom and school. Summarize the difference between teasing and kidding. When does kidding stop being funny? What does it feel like to be teased, and what can be done about it?

Stop the Tease Monster Game

LEARNING OBJECTIVES

Students will:

- practice identifying teasing behaviors
- learn to use I-messages in teasing situations

MATERIALS NEEDED

The book *The Meanest Thing to Say* by Bill Cosby, "Stop the Tease Monster Game" template (page 111) copied onto an overhead transparency, overhead projector, playing piece, coin.

LESSON PLAN

READ *The Meanest Thing to Say*. Little Bill must figure out how to avoid the challenge offered by the new kid in his class, a duel of insults. Bill doesn't want to join in. With his family's help, Bill finds a solution.

DISCUSS What was the problem Bill had to face? Why was it a problem for Bill? What did Bill do to get some help? How did he solve the problem?

DO Play the "Stop the Tease Monster" game. Be sure everyone understands these directions before playing.

- Display the game transparency on the overhead projector. Note that there are 14 teasing situations on the game board.
- Play the game all together in one large group. Later you may want to have teams play each other.
- Flip a coin to proceed along the game path. Heads = move 1 space, Tails = move 2 spaces.
- If you land on a space with a thumbs-up, flip the coin again to go on.
- If you land on a space with the Tease Monster and a word, ask the students: What do we do? They should reply, "Stop the Tease Monster." Discuss and solve the teasing situation indicated by the word.
- If you land on a question mark, students are to provide their own teasing situation and a solution for it.

RELATE what the class learned about kidding and teasing in this lesson to real life. Ask the class if they feel better prepared to deal with teasing. Remind students that in a safe and caring school, everyone is respectful. Teasing someone in a hurtful way is not how we treat others.

It's Okay to Tell Sometimes

LEARNING OBJECTIVES

Students will:

- learn the difference between asking for help and tattling
- discover how to ask for help when dealing with conflict

MATERIALS NEEDED

The book *Telling Isn't Tattling* by Kathryn M. Hammerseng, "It's Okay to Tell Sometimes" activity sheet (page 112), writing tools

LESSON PLAN

READ *Telling Isn't Tattling*. This easy-to-read book describes several situations and asks kids to determine whether the characters are tattling or if they really need an adult to intervene.

An optional text for independent reading or teacher modeled and shared reading is *Speak Up, Chelsea Martin!* by Becky T. Lindberg. Third-grader Chelsea Martin learns to speak up when in conflict with others.

DISCUSS What does it sound like when someone is tattling? What does it sound like when someone is asking for help? What are the differences?

DO the "It's Okay to Tell Sometimes" activity sheet. Students are to create a cartoon about a situation where it is necessary to get an adult's help.

RELATE the lesson to the children's lives by asking them to share their cartoons with the class. Remind students that everyone has a hard time knowing what to do sometimes when we are in conflict situations. Review the difference between asking for help and tattling. Sometimes children will not ask for help out of fear that it may be perceived as tattling and will get them into trouble. Remind students that it takes courage to ask for help, especially if their own attempts to solve a problem did not work.

Courageous and Safe

LEARNING OBJECTIVES

Students will:

- understand the meaning of courage and the different ways people can be courageous
- learn how to be courageous in the face of bullying

MATERIALS NEEDED

The book *The Ant Bully* by John Nickle, "Courageous and Safe" activity sheet (page 113), writing tools

LESSON PLAN

READ   *The Ant Bully*. Ten-year-old Lucas is tormented by a neighborhood bully. He takes out his frustration on the anthill in his yard. The ants decide to teach Lucas a lesson about friendship and having the courage to stand up for himself.

DISCUSS   What happened to Lucas? On whom did he take out his frustrations? Who decided to teach him a lesson and how? What were the two most important things Lucas learned in the story? What is the definition of *courage?* What would be the opposite of courage?

DO   the "Courageous and Safe" activity sheet. Students will write five words that describe courage and use them in sentences that show how to be courageous.

RELATE   the lesson to real-life situations by reviewing the completed activity sheets. What are some examples of times we need to be courageous? When is it safe to stand up to bullying? When is it best to walk away? How do you know the difference?

> *"Safe & Caring Schools is very much a part of everything I do. In my transitional fourth grade classroom, we constantly talk about the choices we make, our interactions with other people, and what results from making good choices versus making choices we would regret in the long run. We talk a lot about personal responsibility, and all of that is so much a part of a safe and caring school."*
>
> TEACHER—SOUTH LAWRENCE EAST SCHOOL

Bullying Quiz

To assess student progress, use the quiz on page 114. (*Answers: 1-F, 2-T, 3-F, 4-T, 5-F, 6-d, 7-b, 8-c, 9-difference, kidding, 10-bystanders, bullies*)

Safe & Caring Vocabulary

Fill in the blanks by unscrambling the words.

Sometimes people _ _ _ _ _ _ to get what they want
ooshce

by being _ _ _ _ _ _ _, but _ _ _ _ – _ _ _ _ _ _ _,
sibleul   meangalncil

_ _ _ _ _ _ _, and _ _ _ _ _ _ _ _ are not the _ _ _ _
netgsia   cevinelo   eafs

and _ _ _ _ _ _ _ _ _ _ _ _ way. We can stop
rgcina   cslohos

bullying when we take the time to _ _ _ _ _ _ _ _ _ _ how
ansdtunrde

someone else _ _ _ _ _. When we try to see
lefse

things from the other person's _ _ _ _, we learn
iwve

to have _ _ _ _ _ _ _ for them and make
hamytep

_ _ _ _ _ _ _ _ choices to help us _ _ _ _ _ _ _ _.
sipeivto   teg gnola

Define the word **empathy**. _____

_____

_____

Write a sentence using the words **positive** and **empathy**.

_____

_____

we aRe
a safe
& CaRiNG
SCHOOL.

SAFE & CARING WORD FIND

Find and circle the words listed at the bottom of the page.
(Hint: Answers can run forward, backward, up, down, or diagonally.)

R	V	F	X	Z	K	R	F	E	E	L	B
K	I	D	D	I	N	G	I	M	A	E	Y
B	E	P	I	T	O	T	U	P	D	U	S
P	S	O	N	A	W	R	A	A	S	O	T
O	C	O	N	F	L	I	C	T	U	R	A
S	C	X	N	S	A	C	R	H	T	R	N
I	O	U	E	R	A	M	M	Y	L	L	D
T	O	N	S	C	Q	C	H	O	O	S	E
I	V	D	S	A	R	O	C	F	G	A	R
V	I	E	W	R	B	U	L	L	I	E	S
E	O	R	H	E	R	R	K	E	P	E	L
N	L	S	R	F	R	A	T	U	R	T	T
G	E	T	J	U	D	G	E	R	I	V	S
I	N	A	Z	L	L	E	L	E	U	O	U
Z	C	N	F	R	I	O	L	U	R	S	R
R	E	D	V	N	G	N	I	S	A	E	T
E	R	C	O	M	P	A	X	X	I	O	N
N	A	M	E	C	A	L	L	I	N	G	M

TATTLE NAME-CALLING KIDDING VIOLENCE
CONFLICT UNDERSTAND COURAGE VIEW
JUDGE KNOW CAREFUL
EMPATHY TRUST POSITIVE
CHOOSE BYSTANDER TELL
BULLIES TEASING FEEL

THE PROBLEM WITH BULLYING

Bullying is _____

_____

_____

_____

Some ways that people bully each other are _____

_____

_____

_____

When I was bullied before, I felt _____

_____

_____

_____

Sometimes I have bullied my:

____ brother, because _____

____ sister, because _____

____ friend, because _____

____ pet, because _____

Some things I can do to stop bullying others are _____

_____

_____

_____

When I see others being hurt by a bully, I can be a positive bystander

_____

_____

we aRe a safe & CaRiNG SCHOOL.

Mean Words Hurt

Sometimes bullies hurt by hitting, other times they hurt by saying mean things.

Sheila thinks Heidi dresses dorky and told her friends not to hang out with Heidi anymore. **How do you think Heidi feels?**

_____
_____
_____

Why do you think Sheila acts so mean? _____
_____
_____

What can Heidi do?

_____
_____
_____

Jack loves to play basketball even though he's not very good. Sam steals the ball and makes fun of how Jack plays. **How do you think Jack feels?**

_____
_____

Why do you think Sam acts so mean?

_____
_____

What can Jack do? _____
_____
_____

WE ARE
a SAFE
& CARiNG
SCHOOL.

A KID'S VIEW ON BULLIES

JANUARY

As we grow up, we see bullies around us. Can you think of examples of bullies...

...in your family? _____
_____
_____
_____
_____

...among your friends? _____
_____
_____
_____
_____

...in movies or on TV? _____
_____
_____
_____
_____

...around your school? _____
_____
_____
_____
_____

...among community leaders? _____
_____
_____
_____
_____

What is a bully anyway? _____
_____
_____
_____
_____
_____
_____

Is it important to resolve conflicts peacefully? Why or why not?
_____
_____
_____
_____
_____
_____

Have you ever been hurt by something a bully said or did?
_____
_____
_____
_____
_____
_____

we are
a safe
& caring
school.

JANUARY

HELPING OUR FRIENDS STOP BULLYING

It's important to learn how we can help each other when we're being bullied.

But we also can help each other **stop being bullies.**

C'mon, let's go tease the new kid!

What can you say or do to help?

_____
_____
_____

It was just a note with a rumor about Jessie... no big deal!

What can you say or do to help?

_____
_____
_____

Write your own...
_____

What can you say or do to help?

_____
_____
_____

we aRe a saFe & CaRiNG SCHOOL.

THE OTHER PERSON'S SHOES

To understand how others feel, it helps to put yourself in their shoes.

Hmm... you mean you have to try to see things from where they stand?

Exactly!

Describe a situation where someone was teased. What happened?	How do you think the person who was teased felt?	What could have been done to help make things better?

What does it take to be a good friend to someone who has been teased?
Write a paragraph about how you can help. _____

_____

_____

_____

_____

_____

WE ARE a SAFE & CARING SCHOOL.

JUST KIDDING!

JANUARY

> **Kidding** can be fun and usually feels okay. But if kidding turns mean, it crosses a line and becomes **teasing**.

List three ways we might kid our friends and then tell how that kidding can turn into teasing.

Kidding: **Teasing:**

The line between kidding and teasing

1 _____   _____

2 _____   _____

3 _____   _____

Tease Tester Are the situations below fun or mean? Use this tester to rate how hurtful or funny each one is by circling the score from 1–5. Is it bullying or not? Explain why.

	Fun				**Mean**	

Calling people names   ① ② ③ ④ ⑤   Is this bullying? Yes or No, explain. _____

Laughing at a joke together   ① ② ③ ④ ⑤   Is this bullying? Yes or No, explain. _____

Pointing and laughing at someone's haircut   ① ② ③ ④ ⑤   Is this bullying? Yes or No, explain. _____

Mimicking someone's speech or accent   ① ② ③ ④ ⑤   Is this bullying? Yes or No, explain. _____

Someone laughing after tripping you   ① ② ③ ④ ⑤   Is this bullying? Yes or No, explain. _____

we aRe a SaFe & CaRiNG SCHOOL.

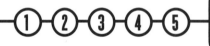
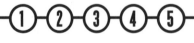
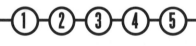
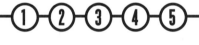
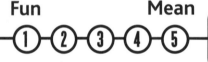

STOP THE TeASe MONSTeR Game

FINISH!

we are a safe & caring school.

Friends

Clothes

Glasses

Name

Shoes

Boyfriend/Girlfriend

Family

Reading

Playing Sports

Drawing

Grades

Hair

Writing

Voice

START

IT'S OKAY TO TELL SOMETIMES

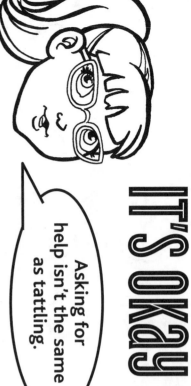

Asking for help isn't the same as tattling.

It's okay to ask for help if you try to solve problems yourself and it doesn't work.

Asking for help takes courage and is a sign of real strength.

Draw a cartoon about a situation you have observed or experienced that required help from an adult. (Include the situation, what happened, how it felt, and who could have helped.)

we are a safe & caring school.

COURAGEOUS AND SAFE

Bullying is not okay, but it's scary to stand up to bullies by yourself.

We need to be courageous **and** safe. That means knowing when to ask for help.

List five words that describe courage:

1) _____

2) _____

3) _____

4) _____

5) _____

Use the five words that describe courage in sentences that show how and when someone can be courageous.

1) _____
_____

2) _____
_____

3) _____
_____

4) _____
_____

5) _____
_____

Okay, real life...

You see a kid being bullied by two other kids, but you're alone. What can you choose to do? How can you be courageous **and** safe?

_____
_____
_____
_____
_____

we aRe a SaFe & CaRiNG SCHOOL.

BULLYING QUIZ

True or False (circle the correct answer)

1) Using mean words or spreading rumors isn't really bullying . . . .**True / False**

2) We can help our friends stop bullying by using Stop, Think, Choose. . . . .**True / False**

3) Girls can't be bullies, only boys are bullies . . . .**True / False**

4) Empathy means we understand how the other person is feeling . . . .**True / False**

5) Bullying isn't a big deal, it's just part of life. . . . .**True / False**

Multiple Choice (circle the correct answer)

6) At a Safe & Caring School:
- **a.** we try not to call each other names or tease.
- **b.** we know bullying is mean and hurts others.
- **c.** we can join together and stop bullying.
- **d.** all of the above

7) One way people bully each other is by:
- **a.** helping clean up the classroom.
- **b.** ignoring somebody because they are different.
- **c.** laughing and joking with friends.
- **d.** making fun of ourselves.

8) It's cool being an ambassador of peace because:
- **a.** I treat others the way I want to be treated.
- **b.** I help stop bullying by helping others who are bullied.
- **c.** I tattle on those I think are bullies.
- **d.** a and b above

Fill in the Blanks

9) There is a big **d**_____ between teasing and **k**_____.

10) When I am a positive **b**_____ , I don't join in with **b**_____ , but I try to help who is being bullied.

Real-Life Writing

When we help others who are bullied, we also need to make sure we stay safe. What can you do if two big bullies follow your friend on the playground and threatened him or her? How can you help your friend without getting yourself into the same trouble with the bullies?

FEBRUARY
Teaming Up for Success

- **Social Interaction Skills**
- **Responsibility**
- **Decision Making**
- **Teamwork**
- **Sharing**

Cooperation is the ability to work well with others in order to get things done. Children need to understand that cooperation is a valuable lifelong skill. We need to teach and model accountability, responsibility, being a good team player, and communicating effectively so they learn that these are all important parts of getting along.

MONTHLY OBJECTIVES
Students will:

- learn the importance of cooperation in all aspects of their lives
- practice the skills of responsibility and accountability
- learn and practice leadership and teamwork skills
- learn and practice communicating effectively with others

TEACHING TIPS

- Cooperation is one skill that takes time to teach. Being part of a team is not always easy for children because they may have a hard time sharing, listening, taking turns, or following directions.
- There are many valuable lessons children can learn while working in large and small groups. Explain to children that they have a right to their own opinions and feelings, even if they differ from the groups.
- Use teachable moments to highlight the importance of good communication and teamwork.

FEBRUARY INTEGRATED ACTIVITIES

In addition to the specific lesson plans for this month, you can use these optional ideas to integrate and extend the Safe & Caring themes into your daily routines and across curricular areas.

LANGUAGE ARTS

- Have students make a list of the responsibilities each family member has at home. Discuss the importance of sharing responsibility.
- Divide students into small groups and ask them to create public announcements about dependability. Make audio recordings of the students' work. Play them over the school's intercom with the morning announcements, or have students make live announcements over the intercom.
- Have students create short commercials about effective communication and videotape them. Celebrate by having a special debut show or play the commercials on video morning announcements.

LITERATURE

- Have students read books based on the theme of cooperation and responsibility, such as *A View for Saturday* by Konigsburg or *Eagle and the Wren* by Jane Goodall. Discuss them, illustrate them, write a new ending, or act out the story.
- Review books on teamwork and responsibility during a Book Review Day. A good book is *The Summer of the Swans* by Betsy Byars.

SOCIAL STUDIES

- Invite community members and parents to talk with students about their particular jobs and their responsibilities.
- Ask students to interview adults to create a list of the skills necessary to successfully complete a task when working as part of a team.
- Research the origin of Valentine's Day. To reinforce the importance of caring for others, distribute Caring Hearts (page 8) as the students make good choices throughout the month.

ART

- Have students draw pictures of the responsibilities they have as students who are part of the classroom team. Collect all pictures and create a booklet titled "We Are a Team."
- Divide students into small groups of four or five and ask them to create a collage that shows people using their cooperation skills to get a job done. For inspiration, read the picture book *The Gigantic Turnip* by Aleksei Tolstoy, a Russian folktale about cooperation.

MUSIC

- Using the song "We Are Family," have students write additional lyrics describing how the concept of family can be extended to include everyone in a classroom, school, neighborhood, or community. For a downloadable teacher's guide that addresses the themes in the song go to www.wearefamilyfoundation.org.

MATH

- Read the book *Pizza Counting* by Christina Dobson. Practice the math concepts and have fun as a team creating a giant pizza out of paper, complete with toppings.

Safe & Caring Vocabulary and Word Find

LEARNING OBJECTIVES

Students will:

- be introduced to the vocabulary that supports learning how to team up for success in a safe and caring classroom
- internalize the vocabulary as they use it throughout the month and year in real-life situations

MATERIALS NEEDED

"Safe & Caring Vocabulary" (page 123) and "Safe & Caring Word Find" (page 124) activity sheets, dictionaries, pencils

LESSON PLAN

Use the vocabulary activities to introduce the concepts and common language associated with this month's theme. Throughout the month, use the words in writing, spelling, storytelling, and dealing with conflict situations.

For "Safe & Caring Schools Vocabulary," explain how to choose the correct word from the word bank to decipher the message. (Doing a _project_ with our friends requires _teamwork_. This involves everyone _sharing_ their _ideas_ and _creativity_ as they _plan_ how to work _together_. The best _teams_ have good _communication_, and all members share _responsibility_ for the work needed to _accomplish_ the team's _goal_. When teammates are _accountable_ and _considerate_ with each other, a team has good _cooperation_ and can achieve _success_.)

For "Safe & Caring Word Find" discuss what the words mean after completing the page. You may want students to work in pairs to help each other.

Responsibility Rocks!

LEARNING OBJECTIVES

Students will:

- learn that responsibility and dependability are part of cooperation
- identify situations where they use cooperation

MATERIALS NEEDED

The book _Dealing with Choices_ by Elizabeth Vogel, "Responsibility Rocks!" activity sheet (page 125), writing and drawing tools, dictionaries

LESSON PLAN

READ   _Dealing with Choices_. The book discusses the importance of choices and how to go about making wise choices.

An option for independent reading or teacher modeled and shared reading is _The Landry News_ by Andrew Clements. A young girl writes a school newspaper story that motivates a worn-out teacher to do a better job. Little did the girl know how much trouble she was creating.

DISCUSS   What is the definition of _responsibility (following through with what one has to do)_ and _dependability (being able to count on one another)_? Discuss how dependability and responsibility are a big part of cooperation and how everyone needs to do their part for things to get done. Ask students what responsibilities they have at home, in the neighborhood, and at school (for example, do homework, help clean up the neighborhood, help with chores).

DO   the "Responsibility Rocks!" activity sheet. Children respond to various scenes calling for responsible action.

RELATE   the activity to how cooperation affects what is accomplished in the classroom. Where would the class be if no one cooperated? Tell students that you expect them to be responsible, dependable, and cooperative in class.

Portrait of a Leader

LEARNING OBJECTIVES

Students will:

- learn the definition of leadership
- identify intelligent qualities of leadership that they possess, both cognitive and emotional

MATERIALS NEEDED

The book *Speak Up and Get Along!* by Scott Cooper, copies of "Portrait of a Leader" activity sheet (page 126), dictionaries, writing and drawing tools

LESSON PLAN

READ   a chapter from *Speak Up and Get Along!* This book provides 21 strategies kids can use to express themselves, build relationships, end arguments and fights, halt bullying, and beat unhappy feelings.

An option for independent reading or teacher modeled and shared reading is *Frindle* by Andrew Clements. When Nick Allen tricks his teacher with a new word, he unwittingly invents a phenomenon that gets blown out of proportion.

DISCUSS   Have students define and create a sentence with the words "leader" or "leadership." Brainstorm qualities they think are the most important for a leader, including emotional, intellectual, and social skills.

DO   the "Portrait of a Leader" activity sheet. Students create a portrait of the leader that is inside of them. Around the outside of the drawing, students write the qualities they have that a leader needs.

RELATE   leadership skills to school and classroom skills. Discuss examples of how they can use their leadership skills at home, at school, and in their community. Ask students to think of other kids at school they consider leaders. Without naming them, ask students to list the characteristics those kids have that make them leaders. Share the portraits from the activity sheets, and have students discuss similarities and differences they have as leaders. You may want to create a "Portraits of Leaders" classroom book with the completed activity sheets.

Cooperation and Me

LEARNING OBJECTIVES

Students will:

- learn about the meaning of cooperation
- discuss the advantages of cooperating in a group to complete a task

MATERIALS NEEDED

The book *Pitch In! Kids Talk About Cooperation* by Pamela Hill Nettleton, "Cooperation and Me" activity sheet (page 127), dictionaries, writing and drawing tools, scissors, construction paper, glue, tape

LESSON PLAN

READ   *Pitch In! Kids Talk About Cooperation*. Using an advice column format, the book pairs handwritten letters from fictional kids with typewritten responses from 13-year-old advice columnist, Frank B. Wize. Many of the questions relate to issues about cooperation and consideration.

An optional text for independent reading or teacher modeled and shared reading is *Locked in the Library!* by Marc Brown. Two friends who are not speaking to each other find they must set aside their differences and work together.

DISCUSS   Do you see yourself more as a leader or a follower when you work on a group project? What is the toughest part about working in a group? What is the easiest?

DO   Assign students to small groups. Give each group the task of creating a model of a new insect. It must have a name and all the essential parts of an insect. Everyone in the small group needs to be involved in creating the creature, and each person will need to report something about the insect to the whole class. Once the bugs are complete, ask students to use dictionaries to define the word *cooperation* and then complete the remaining questions on the "Cooperation and Me" activity sheet.

RELATE   Have the groups report on their bug creations. Then discuss what they learned about cooperation in the group process. Decide which persons in the group acted more like leaders and which were followers. If someone in the group didn't work cooperatively, how was that dealt with? What is the toughest part about working in a group? What are the advantages to working cooperatively in a group?

Teamwork Means Everybody!

LEARNING OBJECTIVES

Students will:

- learn that responsibility is a part of cooperation and that they are responsible for their own actions
- practice using cooperation skills

MATERIALS NEEDED

The book *Teamwork* by Ann Morris, "Teamwork Means Everybody!" activity sheet (page 128), writing and drawing tools.

LESSON PLAN

READ *Teamwork.* This book uses photos to illustrate the concept of teamwork, showing children a fresh view of people working and playing together.

DISCUSS As a class, define *team (group working together to accomplish a common goal)*, *responsibility (following through with what you have to do)*, and *dependability (being able to count on each other)*. Brainstorm ways to be responsible, and discuss the importance of being dependable to others and yourself. Explain to students that when they are part of a team, they are responsible to share the work so things get done well and on time. If they expect to share the credit for the work the team does, they need to contribute. Ask students to give you examples of successful teamwork.

DO the "Teamwork Means Everybody!" activity. Students work in small groups to create a cartoon about teamwork. Use blank sheets of paper to concept and draw a first draft of the cartoon before using the activity sheet for the final work. Break down the project into small steps, answering these questions:

- Step One: What will each team member do? Who can be the writer and who can be the illustrator?

- Step Two: What is the story line? What cartoon characters will be used? What are their names?

- Step Three: What story are you going to tell? What happened? How is teamwork demonstrated in the cartoon?

RELATE Use the cartoons and the process to create them to identify key components of teamwork, responsibility, and dependability. How does this relate to the students' everyday lives? Ask students what they learned about teamwork from this activity.

Test Your Teamwork

LEARNING OBJECTIVES

Students will:

- learn to cooperate and solve problems in teams
- practice sharing and taking turns

MATERIALS NEEDED

The book *City Green* by DyAnne DiSalvo-Ryan, "Test Your Teamwork" activity sheet (page 129), scissors, envelopes

LESSON PLAN

READ *City Green.* Young Marcy is saddened after the city condemns and demolishes a building in her neighborhood. This is a positive story of cooperation that features multi-ethnic characters as they work together to create an oasis in the city on the dirty vacant lot.

An optional text for independent reading or teacher modeled and shared reading is *School Story* by Andrew Clements. A gifted young writer teams up with her best friend to get a book published. Though the challenges are daunting, the two-girl team proves that people working together can accomplish amazing things.

DISCUSS how Marcy and Miss Rosa worked together to beautify the vacant lot. What did the vacant lot project do for Marcy's neighborhood? What can groups do that individuals can't?

DO Make copies of and cut out the puzzle pieces from the "Test Your Teamwork" activity sheet. Keep the three different puzzles separate. Distribute all three puzzles to each small group of students. Students work together to solve the puzzles by creating one word from each set of pieces.

For more challenge, ask students to work in silence, or see how fast they can complete all three puzzles, or have each group create their own puzzle and give it to another group to solve.

RELATE this activity to daily life by asking students to describe the dynamics of their group. Ask: How did they work as a team? Did they take turns sharing ideas? Did they give an opportunity to everyone to participate in putting the puzzles together? Ask the students to share specific ways cooperation helped their group. Celebrate and support the class for their efforts to cooperate in teams.

Making Decisions

LEARNING OBJECTIVES

Students will:

- define the word "decision" and compare easy and hard decisions.

- learn about the importance of decision-making, both individually and in the context of a family or team.

MATERIALS NEEDED

The book *Christina Katerina and the Time She Quit the Family* by Patricia Lee Gauch, "Decision Making" activity sheet (page 130), writing tools, dictionary

LESSON PLAN

READ   *Christina Katerina and the Time She Quit the Family.* When Christina is unfairly blamed in the family, she decides to quit the family. Even though she has fun at first, Christina discovers just how much she misses and needs her family.

An optional text for independent reading or teacher modeled and shared reading is *Stories Julian Tells* by Ann Cameron. Julian tells magnificent stories, but they aren't always true, and they cause him some trouble.

DISCUSS   Why did Christina want to quit the family? What was her decision based on? Was she happy with her decision? What were the good and bad things about her decision? What happens when we make decisions without thinking through the consequences? Should we make tough decisions without some guidance? Who can we ask for help?

DO   the "Decision Making" activity sheet. Have students write a definition for "decision" and then rank each decision as easy, hard, or needs help. The unscrambled words are: *decisions, make, know, tough, help, best.*

RELATE   the topic of decision making to the students' lives. Poll the class on whether or not they thought the situations on the activity sheet were easy or hard. Who wanted help, and with which decisions? What could be the consequences of some of the decisions? Who do you go to for help in making decisions? Let the class know that a teacher can be a source of help.

Sharing in Teams

LEARNING OBJECTIVES

Students will:

- learn what it means to be part of a team and the roles and responsibilities shared in teams
- evaluate their experiences in a team setting

MATERIALS NEEDED

The book *We Are a Team* by Sharon Gordon, "Sharing in Teams" activity sheet (page 131), writing tools, writing paper, books the class has read together in recent weeks

LESSON PLAN

READ   *We Are a Team.* This book demonstrates the importance of teamwork.

DISCUSS   What makes a great team? In what ways did the team in the story share their responsibilities and their talents? How did they help each other to make sure they had a good team? If you belong on a sports team, what do you like most and least? What would you like to change?

DO   the "Sharing in Teams" activity sheet. Create teams of three to five students. Each team must complete the following task as quickly as possible. Once the task is finished, the students are to complete the activity sheet explaining how they felt about the process. Then have fun presenting and watching the frame dramas.

> *Task:* Each group is to tell the story of one of the books they recently read using a frame drama—a sequence of still frames. The group members play the characters of the book, as they arrange themselves with facial and body expressions in scenes to tell the story. No dialog may be used, and the group must use 10 or fewer scenes to tell the whole story. Allow sufficient time for the groups to select a story and prepare the frame drama.

RELATE   this experience to the value of working together on a team. Review the answers to the activity sheet. Did the groups work together as teams? What types of responsibilities do people have when they belong on a team? Do people ever argue or disagree about the role or power they have as a team member? Are there times when not everyone shares responsibility of what needs to be done? In that case, what happens to the team?

A Great Team!

LEARNING OBJECTIVES

Students will:

- learn how good teams can accomplish great things when they combine their efforts and talents
- explore and list the individual qualities of its membership that, when combined, will help make an effective team

MATERIALS NEEDED

The book *The Giant Turnip* by Henriette Barkow, "A Great Team" activity sheet (page 132), writing tools

LESSON PLAN

READ   *The Giant Turnip*. The children have grown an enormous turnip, but they cannot harvest it. They think of various methods to try, but none of them work. With the addition of one more person and everyone working as a team, they finally get the job done.

An optional text, if you want to get your students active in teamwork and community service, is *The Kid's Guide to Service Projects* by Barbara A. Lewis. This guide has something for everyone who wants to make a difference, from simple projects to large-scale commitments.

DISCUSS   In the story, what was the turning point for finding a way to harvest the giant turnip? Ask students to brainstorm words associated with what makes a great team. Review the definitions of the words and use them as a guide to assist with the following activity.

DO   "A Great Team!" activity sheet. Place students in teams of six or less, making sure there is an even number of teams. Each team needs one activity sheet. Complete the top section by recording each person's best qualities for teamwork (for example: artistic, smart, good handwriting, strong, organized, creative). The team then chooses one quality from each team member to make a composite team profile. When done, pair one team with another to compare and record similarities and differences.

RELATE   this experience to team building. What did students discover about their team members that surprised them? What did they not know? What are the differences and similarities in skills and strengths between teams? What qualities of a great team are important for continued success in school and life?

All Together Now

LEARNING OBJECTIVES

Students will:

- identify ways to be more accepting of people with different abilities
- compile data on the class, evaluate how inclusive they are as a classroom, and use graphs to process the data

MATERIALS NEEDED

The book *Oliver Onion: The Onion Who Learns to Accept and Be Himself* by Diane Murrell, "All Together Now" activity sheet (page 133), writing tools

LESSON PLAN

READ   *Oliver Onion*. Oliver learns that our differences make us unique. This book presents many opportunities for sharing feelings and thoughts about understanding and self-acceptance.

An optional text for independent reading or teacher modeled and shared reading is *Rules* by Cynthia Lord. This story is about being different, feeling different, and finding acceptance.

DISCUSS   the many ways we can be different. How was Oliver different? Make a list of student responses. Be sure to include physical, cultural, and intellectual differences. How can the class make sure that everyone feels included and special despite their varying abilities or needs?

DO   the "All Together Now" activity sheet. Students answer true or false questions about inclusion, and then they calculate the results. This sheet may be done as a whole group activity on an overhead projector. Graph the results on the board or poster board.

RELATE   how it feels to be left out to how others may be feeling in school or in the community. Why do people choose to exclude others from activities, events, or teams? Take a vote to find out how accepting and inclusive the class is, and then discuss what might be done differently to improve the situation.

Leaders and Followers

LEARNING OBJECTIVES

Students will:

- discuss the difference between leading and being bossy
- determine, on a continuum, whether they are more like leaders or like followers

MATERIALS NEEDED

The book *The Berenstain Bears and the Trouble with Friends* by Stan & Jan Berenstain, "Leaders and Followers" activity sheet (page 134), writing tools

LESSON PLAN

READ   *The Berenstain Bears and the Trouble with Friends*, a children's story with a message for everyone. The new cub in the neighborhood, Lizzy Bruin, is the same age as Sister Bear, and she's also just as bossy. After a fight threatens their budding friendship, both cubs learn that you can't always have your own way if you want to have friends.

> An optional text for a more in-depth study of leadership characteristics is *What Do You Stand For? For Kids* by Barbara A. Lewis. True stories, thought-provoking dilemmas, and activities help elementary school kids build positive character traits, including caring, fairness, respect, and responsibility.

DISCUSS   What is the difference between being a leader and being bossy? What were the cubs' problems in the story? What characteristics does a leader have? How can you use your leadership skills to influence others in a positive way?

DO   the "Leaders and Followers" activity sheet. Students rate themselves to determine if they tend to be more like leaders or like followers.

RELATE   what students learned about themselves to working in teams within the classroom. Ask: What are the qualities of a positive leader? Can you choose to be a leader and a follower at different times? What are some ways leaders can be a great example of a follower? Do you usually follow along with whatever the group wants to do, even if you disagree? Why or why not?

"Safe & Caring Schools lends itself very easily to classroom use; it's so teacher friendly. You just pull from the materials and it opens another door for students to discover their own roles in the classroom, to have voices within themselves, and to share that with everyone else. It helps to promote an understanding of the community."

TEACHER—JOHN BREEN SCHOOL

Teaming Up for Success Quiz

To assess student progress, use the quiz on page 135. (Answers: 1-T, 2-F, 3-F, 4-F, 5-T, 6-c, 7-d, 8-d, 9-strengths, 10-important, team)

SAFE & CARING VOCABULARY

Fill in the blanks below with the correct words from the list.

communication
success
plan
teamwork
project

sharing
ideas
cooperation
accomplish
considerate
together

teams
responsibility
goal
accountable
creativity

Doing a _ _ _ _ _ _ _ with our friends requires
_ _ _ _ _ _ _ _. This involves everyone _ _ _ _ _ _ _
their _ _ _ _ _ and _ _ _ _ _ _ _ _ _ _ as they_ _ _ _
how to work _ _ _ _ _ _ _ _. The best_ _ _ _ _ have
good _ _ _ _ _ _ _ _ _ _ _ _ _, and all members share
_ _ _ _ _ _ _ _ _ _ _ _ _ for the work needed to
_ _ _ _ _ _ _ _ _ _ the team's _ _ _ _. When teammates
are _ _ _ _ _ _ _ _ _ _ _ and_ _ _ _ _ _ _ _ _ _ with
each other, a team has good_ _ _ _ _ _ _ _ _ _ _
and can achieve _ _ _ _ _ _ _.

Define the word **cooperation**. _____

_____

_____

How does cooperation make teamwork easier?

_____

_____

we are
a safe
& caring
school.

SAFE & CARING WORD FIND

Find and circle the words listed at the bottom of the page.
(Hint: Answers can run forward, backward, up, down, or diagonally.)

C	R	E	A	T	I	V	I	T	Y	P	V
O	C	T	O	G	E	T	H	E	R	X	Z
M	O	E	T	P	O	P	H	A	B	W	R
M	N	T	G	A	T	M	E	M	B	E	R
U	S	U	C	C	E	S	S	W	E	L	E
N	I	R	K	L	A	P	P	O	P	O	S
I	D	E	A	S	M	S	E	R	U	P	P
C	E	D	C	H	S	A	R	K	D	R	O
A	R	I	C	A	E	C	I	S	I	O	N
T	A	S	O	R	R	C	L	H	S	J	S
I	T	N	U	I	S	O	L	A	C	E	I
O	E	O	N	N	H	M	P	R	U	C	B
N	T	C	T	G	I	P	V	I	S	T	I
P	Y	P	A	G	P	L	A	G	O	A	L
Y	L	T	B	N	P	I	J	G	I	H	I
R	P	P	L	A	N	S	P	N	O	A	T
D	C	Q	E	N	D	H	Q	P	N	J	Y
S	C	O	O	P	E	R	A	T	I	O	N

GOAL	COMMUNICATION	ACCOUNTABLE
PLAN	PROJECT	SHARING
IDEAS	SUCCESS	TOGETHER
TEAMS	CREATIVITY	ACCOMPLISH
TEAMWORK	COOPERATION	
RESPONSIBILITY	CONSIDERATE	

we are a safe & caring school.

RESPONSIBILITY ROCKS!

I act responsibly in my classroom by _____

_____

_____

_____

_____

_____

I'm responsible for my own actions!

I act responsibly with my friends by _____

_____

_____

_____

_____

_____

I act responsibly in my family by _____

_____

_____

_____

_____

I act responsibly to myself by _____

_____

_____

_____

_____

we are a safe & caring school.

PORTRAIT OF A LEADER

Everybody has a leader inside of them. Describe leadership qualities you have and draw your self-portrait.

Leadership Quality #1

Leadership Quality #2

Leadership Quality #3

A leader is someone who...

As a leader, what would you like to do?

COOPERATION & ME

Cooperation means...

_____
_____
_____
_____
_____
_____
_____

Name something it takes a group to do.

What do people do when they cooperate?

_____
_____
_____
_____
_____

_____
_____
_____
_____

What problems are caused when people don't cooperate?

Why is it always good to cooperate?

_____
_____
_____

we are a safe & caring school.

Teamwork means Everybody!

WE ARE
A SAFE
& CARING
SCHOOL.

TEST YOUR TEAMWORK

RESPONSIBILITY

COOPERATION

ACCOUNTABILITY

we are a safe & caring school.

DECISION MAKING

Define decision: _____

Some decisions are easier to make than others.

Look at each decision below and decide if it's easy or hard or if you might need help to make that decision.

1) Go to the movies or wash the dishes?
☐ Easy   ☐ Hard   ☐ Help!

2) Which clothes should I wear to the party?
☐ Easy   ☐ Hard   ☐ Help!

3) Chicken or potato chips for dinner?
☐ Easy   ☐ Hard   ☐ Help!

4) Which friend should I play with?
☐ Easy   ☐ Hard   ☐ Help!

5) Which book should I read for my report?
☐ Easy   ☐ Hard   ☐ Help!

6) Do I tell the teacher my friend is being picked on?
☐ Easy   ☐ Hard   ☐ Help!

Unscramble the words below for a great tip about decision making.

We all have _ _ _ _ _ _ _ _ _ to _ _ _ _.
c i s d e o n s i   e a k m

Sometimes we _ _ _ _ exactly what to
w o n k

do. Other times, it is _ _ _ _ _ to decide.
h u g o t

Sometimes we might even need _ _ _ _
l e p h

to make the _ _ _ _ _ choices.
s e b t

WE ARE
A SAFE
& CARING
SCHOOL.

SHARING IN TEAMS

When you're part of a team, you do some things as a group and some things individually.

But to get more done, you need to share some of the workload and responsibilities.

What duties did the team assign?

_____
_____
_____
_____
_____
_____
_____
_____
_____

What worked well with your team?

_____
_____
_____
_____
_____
_____
_____
_____
_____
_____

Were team members asked for suggestions?

_____
_____
_____
_____
_____
_____
_____
_____
_____

Why was, or wasn't, the team successful?

_____
_____
_____
_____
_____
_____
_____
_____
_____

Our Team

What didn't work well?

_____
_____
_____
_____
_____
_____
_____
_____
_____
_____

What would you change about your team?

_____
_____
_____
_____
_____
_____
_____
_____
_____

WE ARE a SAFE & CARiNG SCHOOL.

A good team uses the best qualities of its members to get things done.

A GREAT TEAM

List the positive qualities of your team members that make your team work well together.

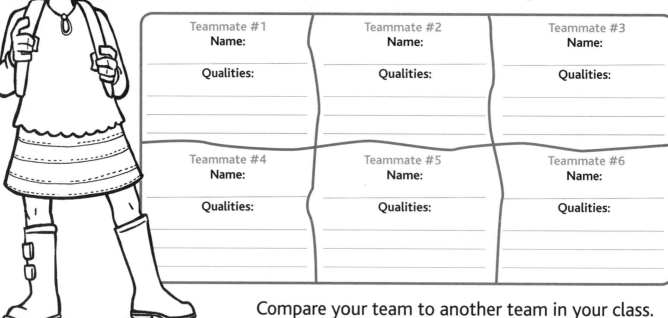

Teammate #1 Name:	Teammate #2 Name:	Teammate #3 Name:
Qualities:	Qualities:	Qualities:
Teammate #4 Name:	Teammate #5 Name:	Teammate #6 Name:
Qualities:	Qualities:	Qualities:

Compare your team to another team in your class.

Team Similarities | **Team Differences**

Team Profile
List one quality or strength of each team member to create a team profile.

we are a safe & caring school.

ALL TOGETHER NOW

Everyone has something to contribute.

Some of our friends have special needs. How can we make sure we include them in our team?

I can choose to include my friends with special needs by:

Inclusion/Exclusion Survey
Answer the following True or False questions:

Now, let's see how the whole class answered.
Total the True and False answers, convert each total to a percentage of students in class, and chart on a graph.

Class totals

0% 20% 40% 60% 80% 100%

1. Everybody feels left out sometimes. T — **24** = — **80** %
   F — **6** = — **20** %

2. It's okay to have alone time. T = %
   F = %

3. It's okay to exclude people if they're different from you. T = %
   F = %

4. It's important to let others know when you feel left out. T = %
   F = %

5. If you're popular, you can exclude anyone you want. T = %
   F = %

6. If you don't know someone, you should exclude them. T = %
   F = %

Survey Conclusions: Write your final conclusions about how students feel about including everyone in classroom teamwork.

we are a safe & caring school.

LEADERS & FOLLOWERS

Sometimes we **lead** and sometimes we **follow** others.

Whether we lead or follow, the important thing is we believe in ourselves and do the right thing.

Read the right and left statements below and rate where you are on the scale.

I like to be the one to come up with ideas for the group.	①②③④⑤	I like to hear what everyone else has to say first.
I almost always start the discussion in my group.	①②③④⑤	I am usually the last person to say something in my group.
I love working in groups.	①②③④⑤	I prefer to work alone.
I make sure we get things done on time.	①②③④⑤	I usually need someone to remind me to get things done.
I like to help the group solve problems.	①②③④⑤	I don't like to get in the middle of conflicts.
I like making my own decisions.	①②③④⑤	I allow others to decide things for me.
I know what I like and what I believe in.	①②③④⑤	I only like what other people like.
When someone tries to get me in trouble, I do the right thing.	①②③④⑤	I usually go along with the group, even if it doesn't feel right.

Based on your answers above, are you more of a leader or a follower? Explain.

_____

_____

_____

we aRe a safe & caRiNG SCHOOL.

Teaming Up For Success QUIZ

True or False (circle the correct answer)

1) Sometimes we need to work in a team to accomplish something we are not able to do on our own. . . . .**True / False**

2) I don't have to be responsible for my part in a team. Someone else will do the work if I don't . . . .**True / False**

3) Being a leader means you get to boss people around. . . . .**True / False**

4) It's no big deal to exclude a teammate you don't like . . . .**True / False**

5) Everyone on a team can have different responsibilities but the same goal. . . . .**True / False**

Multiple Choice (circle the correct answer)

6) At a Safe & Caring School:
   - **a.** working in teams is too hard, because nobody gets along together.
   - **b.** we know nothing can be accomplished even when we cooperate.
   - **c.** everyone can try out their leadership skills.
   - **d.** the bossy one gets to be the leader.

7) Peer pressure in teams:
   - **a.** can help move things along.
   - **b.** can spoil the mood and keep people from participating.
   - **c.** can be both positive or negative.
   - **d.** all of the above

8) Cooperation requires:
   - **a.** caring.
   - **b.** dependability.
   - **c.** responsibility.
   - **d.** all of the above

Fill in the Blanks

9) A great team uses its **s**_____ to get work done.

10) Good communication is **i**_____ to keep a **t**_____ working well together.

Real-Life Writing

You are on a team where the leader takes things too far and is too bossy. Some others on the team aren't doing their jobs, and the work isn't getting done. What can you say or do to help the team get going?

we are
a safe
& caring
school.

MARCH
Conflict Resolution

- **Active Listening**

- **Self-Control**

- **Respectful Communication**

- **Getting Along with Others**

Because conflict is part of everyday life, students need to recognize anger signals and learn how to deal with differences in nonviolent ways. To do this, they can practice their listening skills and develop the ability to negotiate and compromise.

MONTHLY OBJECTIVES
Students will:

- understand what conflict is, how it escalates, and how to respond to it assertively

- learn to use negotiating skills to resolve conflicts peacefully

TEACHING TIPS

- Give your students a few minutes of individual attention each day.
- Show students how to ask for attention in appropriate ways.
- Recognize children every time they make a good choice.
- Find ways to give every student a chance to succeed.

In addition to the specific lesson plans for this month, you can use these ideas to integrate and extend the Safe & Caring themes into your daily routines and across curricular areas.

LANGUAGE ARTS

- Write or draw pictures in journals about conflicts students managed to resolve in peaceful ways.

- Review articles that deal with local, national, or international conflict. Have brainstorming sessions to come up with solutions for each conflict.

- Create poems or short stories using words and/or pictures that show conflicts being resolved in positive ways.

LITERATURE

- Read short stories about people around the world who made a difference by promoting peace. Use *The Big Book for Peace* edited by Ann Durell and Marilyn Sachs as a resource.

- Have students read and review books that involve conflict (for example, *How to Survive Third Grade* by Laurie Lawlor). Discuss how the characters felt during the conflict, how they dealt with tough situations, and how they chose to resolve the problem.

- Have students re-create stories by writing short skits to present to the class. Ask them to end the skits with positive solutions to the conflict.

SOCIAL STUDIES

- Discuss different kinds of conflict that happen at home, in communities, at schools, around the country, or in the world. Brainstorm ways to resolve these conflicts peacefully.

- Have students create timelines showing how a minor disagreement or misunderstanding can turn into an argument, which then turns into a major conflict. Discuss ways to prevent conflict from getting out of control.

- Define *attitude* and discuss its different meanings. Discuss attitudes people have toward different cultures, ideas, beliefs, music, or customs. What does it mean to have a negative attitude? What does it mean to have a positive attitude?

- Study people from history who had positive attitudes and how they affected those around them.

ART

- The dove is used often as a symbol for peace. Make paper doves to hang from the ceiling and add words of peace or ways students can help promote peace in school.

- Create posters that show peaceful ways to deal with conflict. Decorate the cafeteria, hallways, or bulletin boards.

- Create collages or murals for the hallways showing the steps people can take to resolve conflict.

MUSIC

- Explore how different instrumental music or melodies can evoke a sense of peacefulness or create tension and conflict. Look for songs that focus on the theme of peace and harmony.

MATH

- Create a survey about ways to resolve conflict. Administer the survey to other students at different grade levels. Graph the results by type of resolution used by grade levels.

- Provide students with real-life situations that require math skills to solve the conflict. (For example, you and your friends buy a pizza. You realize that there are 12 pieces of pizza and 5 kids. Negotiate a way to divide the pizza that is fair for everyone.)

Safe & Caring Vocabulary and Word Find

LEARNING OBJECTIVES

Students will:

- be introduced to vocabulary that supports learning how to get along with others
- internalize the vocabulary as they use it throughout the month and year in real life situations

MATERIALS NEEDED

"Safe & Caring Vocabulary" (page 143) and "Safe & Caring Word Find" (page 144) activity sheets, pencils, dictionaries

LESSON PLAN

Use the vocabulary activities to introduce the concepts and common language associated with this month's theme. Throughout the month, use the words in writing, spelling, storytelling, and dealing with conflict situations.

For "Safe & Caring Schools Vocabulary," explain how to use the secret code to decipher the message. (Kids who learn how to *stop*, *think*, *choose* can solve *conflicts peacefully*. They know it is best not to *interrupt*, but instead, use *active* *listening* to help them *understand* what the *problem* is. When someone is being *aggressive*, *safe* and *caring* kids know what to do. They have the choice to be *passive* and do nothing or *assertive* and use *I-messages* to *resolve* the *conflict* with *respect*.)

For "Safe & Caring Word Find," discuss what the words mean after completing the page. You may want students to work in pairs to help each other.

```
K R E S O L V E I O N K
O E U N D E R S T A N D
A S D G C H O O S E K Y
I P C O H P A B C Z M O
A E C I O T H I N K K P
S C C O O I S E Y L E R
S T O P N Q X V E G N O
E B N Z E L A I M Z P B
R U F C B L I T Q E P L
T L L A A R N C A K P E
I L I R F S S A T E E M
V Y C I P E A K E R A S
E A T N T P Z B A K C O
O A G G R E S S I V E L
J N R K M E N A C R F V
T H I P A S S I V E U I
R O I V A H E B N G L N
I N T L I S T E N I N G
```

Totally Listening

LEARNING OBJECTIVES

Students will:

- understand why it is important to listen
- learn the steps of being an active listener

MATERIALS NEEDED

The book *The Surprise Party* by Pat Hutchins, "Totally Listening" activity sheet (page 145), and colored pencils, crayons, or markers

LESSON PLAN

READ   *The Surprise Party*. This is a fable about how one animal's message gets so mixed up as it is passed from one animal to the next. The only thing the animals know for sure is that everybody has the wrong story.

DISCUSS   Why is it important to listen? How does listening help us get things done right? What can happen between friends when someone doesn't listen? How do you feel when people choose not to listen to you?

DO   Review the steps for being a good listener on the "Totally Listening" activity sheet. Have children share examples of when they were a good listener and when they had problems listening. What made it easy to listen one time but hard another? Color the sheet for display throughout the school.

RELATE   the importance of good listening in everything we do by playing the telephone game. Stand in a circle. Whisper a message into the ear of the student on your right; only say it once. Have each student pass the message around the circle by whispering it one time into the ear of the next person. Have the last person in the circle say the message aloud. The message is likely not the same thing you whispered to the first student. Discuss how well the message was passed from person to person and how easy it is to hear the wrong thing. Sometimes arguments start because of such simple misunderstandings. Remind the class that they should be practicing good listening skills every day.

Listen Up!

LEARNING OBJECTIVES

Students will:

- associate being a good and a poor listener to their behavior
- learn about active listening and the consequences of not being an active listener

MATERIALS NEEDED

The book *My Momma Likes to Say* by Denise Brennan-Nelson, "Listen Up!" activity sheet (page 146), writing and drawing tools, drawing paper

LESSON PLAN

READ *My Momma Likes to Say*. This book has visual interpretations of idioms and witticisms, including "Hold your horses" and "I have eyes in the back of my head." Students will learn about the concepts of taking things literally versus listening carefully for the true meaning behind the words.

DISCUSS Explain how active listening helps us get our work done, solve problems, and share what we are thinking and feeling with our friends. Review the phrases from the book and discuss their meanings. (English language learners will likely need the idioms explained.) Explore the concept of using creative writing to express an idea in the same way the author has done in the book.

DO the "Listen Up!" activity sheet. Students write ways they can be better listeners and respond to true or false questions about listening.

As an activity extension, ask students to choose one of their favorite sayings from the book and create their own artistic interpretation of it. Use the students' artwork to create a classroom book of visual idioms.

RELATE active listening to student performance. Review the completed activity sheets in class. Emphasize that active listening includes paying attention to the meanings of words. Do you think better listening could improve your work in all school subjects?

Get the Whole Story

LEARNING OBJECTIVES

Students will:

- learn to pay attention to story details
- practice listening for accuracy and reporting what they hear

MATERIALS NEEDED

The book *My Teacher Likes to Say* by Denise Brennan-Nelson, "Get the Whole Story" activity sheet (page 147), writing and drawing tools

LESSON PLAN

READ *My Teacher Likes to Say*. The book contains visual interpretations of idioms and witticisms, including "Do you have ants in your pants?" "Stick together!" and "Great minds think alike." Use this as a tool to help kids listen for understanding.

DISCUSS Do the idioms always make sense to you? Which ones need more explanation? Read an idiom from the book and have students repeat it to you. This takes careful listening for the details. Try more idioms to improve the skill of listening for details. Ask the students why it is important to pay attention to details.

DO the "Get the Whole Story" activity sheet. Prepare the sheets ahead of time by cutting them into the three parts. Have students work in teams of two, and give each partner one of the two stories. Students are to only look at the story they have been given. Give both partners a copy of the "Active Listening Practice Sheet" from the bottom of the activity sheet. Have students take turns being the listener while the other person reads the story. After reading the first story aloud, the reader asks the listener the questions about the story and records the answers given on the "Active Listening Practice Sheet." Then the students switch roles and use the second story. See how many questions are answered correctly the first time through the stories. If you have time, read the stories again and try again answering the questions.

RELATE this activity to real-life situations in school. Was it harder to be the reader or the listener? Why? Review the importance of careful listening. Where in school is listening tied directly to your success? Explain that careful listening and accurately reporting information are important skills for school and for life.

Picture This

LEARNING OBJECTIVES

Students will:

- practice giving and following directions
- reflect on the fear of the unknown

MATERIALS NEEDED

The book *Brave as a Mountain Lion* by Ann Herbert Scott, "Picture This" activity sheet (page 148), writing and drawing tools, drawing paper

LESSON PLAN

READ *Brave as a Mountain Lion*. A young boy is afraid to go on stage at the school spelling bee. After listening to his father's advice, he decides he will try to be as brave as his Shoshoni ancestors.

DISCUSS Define the word *brave* and discuss how adults and kids show bravery. *(Answers may include standing up for what they believe in, taking a risk, making a tough choice, helping a friend in trouble, making a difference in the community.)* What unknown things do we sometimes fear? How can we reduce our fear of the unknown?

DO the "Picture This" activity. Prepare the activity sheets in advance by cutting the pages into two parts. Have students work in pairs, sitting back-to-back. Give each partner one part of the activity page, and instruct them to not let the partner see the page. The first partner (the caller) pretends to have a telephone conversation with the second (the listener). The caller describes the diagram on his or her half of the activity sheet. The listener cannot ask questions, and he or she must draw the diagram being described. Once the caller finishes giving directions, compare the actual pattern with the one the listener drew. Then reverse roles and try again.

RELATE what the students learned about attentive listening in the activity to life in the classroom. Ask: Was it easier to give or receive directions? Why? How did you feel during the activity? What might change if the listener was allowed to ask questions? Tell the students that communicating clearly is very important. Never assume that everyone understands what is said. And it is okay to ask questions if something is not understood.

Cool Response

LEARNING OBJECTIVES

Students will:

- re-examine passive, assertive, and aggressive behaviors
- learn the skills for behaving assertively in different conflict situations

MATERIALS NEEDED

The book *I Hate Everyone* by Mij Keller, "Cool Response" activity sheet (page 149), dictionaries, writing and drawing tools, paper

LESSON PLAN

READ *I Hate Everyone*. Queen Bee is not having a good day, and everyone knows it. When ordering others to fetch everything from ice cream to huckleberry pies, she never, ever says "please."

An optional text for classroom reading is *Stop Picking on Me* by Pat Thomas. When bullies pick on a boy at school, a classmate is afraid, but decides that he must do something.

DISCUSS the different ways the bees in the book are behaving. Talk about the difference between hurtful and respectful words. Ask children how they feel when someone uses unkind words. Who finally tells the Queen what she needs to hear?

DO Divide students into small groups and ask them to define *passive, aggressive,* and *assertive*. Review the definitions and distribute the "Cool Response" activity sheet. Students are to give passive, aggressive, and assertive responses to the listed situations.

- Passive Response: Each time the student chooses not to say or do anything at all.
- Aggressive Response: Each time the student chooses to fight back verbally or physically.
- Assertive Response: The student chooses to

1. Say "stop" and use I-messages.
2. Ask for help from a trusted adult.
3. Walk away and say "no" to any part of the conflict.
4. Patiently wait, or politely hand your mother a note to ask when she might be finished with the phone.

RELATE what the students learned from the activity sheet to what usually happens in their daily lives. Do they most often use passive, aggressive, or assertive responses? What are the consequences for each type of response?

All About Conflict

LEARNING OBJECTIVES

Students will:

- revisit and define *conflict*
- list conflicts seen in different contexts and determine negative and positive responses

MATERIALS NEEDED

The book *The Paper Bag Princess* by Robert N. Munsch, "All About Conflict" activity sheet (page 150), dictionary, writing tools

LESSON PLAN

READ *The Paper Bag Princess*. Just when Princess Elizabeth is about to marry Prince Ronald, a dragon smashes her castle, burns her clothes, and "prince-naps" her dear Ronald. Undaunted and having only a large paper bag for clothing, she sets off to find the dragon and her prince.

DISCUSS What was the conflict in the story? How did Elizabeth handle the conflict? Was she passive, aggressive, or assertive? Remind students that conflict is not always physical; it can be verbal, too.

DO the "All About Conflict" activity sheet. Divide the class into small groups. Working together, have the students each complete an activity sheet. They will define *conflict* and write why they think people have conflicts. Then, they will record conflict they have seen in different locations and the responses they observed to that conflict. Were the responses passive, aggressive, or assertive?

RELATE what the children learned about conflict to daily life at school. Ask: Are you aware of conflicts in the classroom? On the playground? What can be done to help alleviate them? How can you be less aggressive and more assertive?

Who's in Charge of Me?

LEARNING OBJECTIVES

Students will:

- learn the importance of impulse control
- discover ways they can be responsible for the things they say and do

MATERIALS NEEDED

The book *Don't Rant and Rave on Wednesdays! The Children's Anger-Control Book* by Adolph Moser, "Who's in Charge of Me?" activity sheet (page 151), writing tools

LESSON PLAN

READ *Don't Rant and Rave on Wednesdays! The Children's Anger-Control Book*. This book teaches kids how to develop self-control and how to express their anger in positive ways.

DISCUSS How do people usually behave when they get frustrated, upset or angry? What does it mean to be responsible for the things you say and do?

DO the "Who's in Charge of Me?" activity sheet. Have students think of a time they were upset by someone or something. Then, have them write what the issue was, their thoughts about it, their feelings at the time, the choices they had, what they chose to do, and the consequences of their actions.

RELATE this activity to the lives of the students by explaining that when they are upset, they are still in control of and responsible for their own choices. Remind them of the Stop, Think, Choose strategy. In difficult times, it is okay that they stop and take time to think about possible options and consequence so that they can make wise choices.

Special Report

LEARNING OBJECTIVES

Students will:

- review the definition of conflict and why it happens
- research a news story about conflict and share ideas about how the conflict could be solved

MATERIALS NEEDED

The book *Potatoes, Potatoes* by Anita Lobel, "Special Report!" activity sheet (page 152), writing tools

LESSON PLAN

READ *Potatoes, Potatoes*. This is a story of two brothers who become enemies at war. Their wise mother finds a way to turn the fighting into peace.

DISCUSS Why did the brothers have a conflict? Who had a solution to the problem? How was the conflict resolved?

DO the "Special Report!" activity sheet. Students become reporters who use the prompts on the sheet to write about a current conflict in the news. Help them find a story to write about by providing topics of interest from local and national news sources.

RELATE the idea of conflict to family life, reminding the students that conflict occurs everywhere, even in our families. What can you do if your efforts to resolve a conflict in a positive way do not work? What does negotiation mean? How does it work?

Stop, Think, Choose Confidence Cruise

LEARNING OBJECTIVES

Students will:

- explore personal confidence using the steps of Stop, Think, Choose
- discuss specific situations where they need to be confident

MATERIALS NEEDED

The book *Wilma Unlimited: How Wilma Rudolph Became the World's Fastest Woman* by Kathleen Krull, "Stop, Think, Choose Confidence Cruise" activity sheet (page 153), writing tools

LESSON PLAN

READ *Wilma Unlimited.* Wilma was born prematurely and was not expected to live. At an early age, she had polio and struggled to walk. Yet she persevered and became the first American woman to win three gold medals during a single Olympic competition (1960).

DISCUSS Why was Wilma not able to walk? Who supported her and built up her confidence? How did she manage to get to the Olympic games? Was Wilma confident?

DO the "Stop, Think, Choose Confidence Cruise" activity sheet. Students sail their ship through the troubled waters, making choices that build confidence along the way.

RELATE how perseverance and confidence are important every day. Define *perseverance* and ask students for examples they have seen or heard about. Ask: Can you describe different ways you can show confidence? What is the hardest thing to do when faced with tough situations? Is it easier to go along with the crowd than find your own solution? What did you discover about yourself as you sailed to Safe & Caring Schools Island?

Change of Attitude

LEARNING OBJECTIVES

Students will:

- explore how their attitude impacts their choices and actions
- compare positive and negative attitudes

MATERIALS NEEDED

The book *Chocolatina* by Erik Kraft, "Change of Attitude" activity sheet (page 154), writing tools

LESSON PLAN

READ *Chocolatina.* Tina loves chocolate more than anything else. When her health teacher, Mrs. Ferdman, makes the class repeat the mantra, "You are what you eat," Tina wishes it would come true.

> An optional text for independent reading or teacher modeled and shared reading is *Be a Perfect Person in Just Three Days!* by Stephen Manes. Milo decides to change his life dramatically to escape his frustration with friends and family.

DISCUSS Why did Tina want to be chocolate? Was it all she thought it would be? What were the problems? How did her attitude change? Sometimes, the only way to make things better is to change our attitude.

DO the "Change of Attitude" activity sheet. Students will draw their own cartoon, dialogue included, about a time when an attitude adjustment is needed. They may use a real situation or make up the storyline. (For example, a student did not finish her homework and has to stay inside from recess to complete it. She has a bad attitude about missing recess, but how can she change it into a positive attitude?)

RELATE how students' attitudes affect their work in school. Ask: What is *attitude*? When was the last time you had a bad attitude? What were the circumstances? What could have been done to improve the situation? How can positive attitudes help us get what we need and want?

Getting Along with Others Quiz

To assess student progress, use the quiz on page 155. (*Answers: 1-F, 2-F, 3-T, 4-F, 5-T, 6-d, 7-a, 8-b, 9-assertive, 10-conflict, positive*)

Safe & Caring Vocabulary

Use the code to spell the missing words.

a	b	c	d	e	f	g	h	i	j	k	l	m	n	o	p	q	r	s	t	u	v	w	x	y	z

Kids who learn how to _ _ _ _, _ _ _ _ _ _, _ _ _ _ _ _ _ _
can solve _ _ _ _ _ _ _ _ _ _ _ _ _ _ _ _ _.
They know it is best not to _ _ _ _ _ _ _ _ _, but
instead, use _ _ _ _ _ _ _ _ _ _ _ _ _ to help
them _ _ _ _ _ _ _ _ _ _ what the _ _ _ _ _ _ _ is.
When someone is being _ _ _ _ _ _ _ _ _ _, _ _ _ _
and _ _ _ _ _ _ kids know what to do. They have
the choice to be _ _ _ _ _ _ _ and do nothing or
_ _ _ _ _ _ _ _ _ and use _ – _ _ _ _ _ _ _ _ to
the _ _ _ _ _ _ _ with _ _ _ _ _ _.

Define **conflict resolution.** _____

_____

_____

Write a sentence explaining what **aggressive behavior** is.

_____

_____

we are a safe & caring school.

MARCH

Safe & Caring WORD FIND

Find and circle the words listed at the bottom of the page.

(Hint: Answers can run forward, backward, up, down, or diagonally.)

K	R	E	S	O	L	V	E	I	O	N	K	K
O	E	U	N	D	E	R	S	T	A	N	D	D
A	S	D	G	C	H	O	O	S	E	K	Y	
I	P	C	O	H	P	A	B	C	Z	M	O	
A	E	C	I	O	T	H	I	N	K	K	P	
S	C	C	O	O	I	S	E	Y	L	E	R	R
S	T	O	P	N	Q	X	V	E	G	N	O	
E	B	N	Z	E	L	A	I	M	Z	P	B	
R	U	F	C	B	L	I	T	Q	E	P	L	
T	L	L	A	A	R	N	C	A	K	P	E	
I	L	I	R	F	S	S	A	T	E	E	M	
V	Y	C	I	P	E	A	K	E	R	A	S	
E	A	T	N	T	P	Z	B	A	K	C	O	
O	A	G	G	R	E	S	S	I	V	E	L	
J	N	R	K	M	E	N	A	C	R	F	V	
T	H	I	P	A	S	S	I	V	E	U	I	
R	O	I	V	A	H	E	B	N	G	L	N	
I	N	T	L	I	S	T	E	N	I	N	G	

CARING	AGGRESSIVE	RESPECT	PROBLEM SOLVING
STOP	PASSIVE	ACTIVE	PEACEFUL
RESOLVE	CONFLICT	THINK	UNDERSTAND
ASSERTIVE	LISTENING	CHOOSE	BEHAVIOR

TOTALLY LISTENING

I look at the person who is speaking to me.

I pay attention and show respect.

I don't interrupt.

I ask questions to understand and participate.

we are a safe & caring school.

LISTEN UP!

I think paying attention to others is important because...

_____
_____
_____
_____

1 _____
_____
_____
_____

Three things I can do to be a better listener are...

2 _____
_____
_____
_____

3 _____
_____
_____
_____

Listen up to get it . . .

Got it!

T F

Interrupting helps listening. . . . . ▢ ▢

Paying attention shows respect. . . . . ▢ ▢

Everyone is a good listener. . . . . ▢ ▢

You don't need to listen to do well at school. . . . . ▢ ▢

There's no need to listen to directions to be
able to do things right. . . . . ▢ ▢

we aRe a saFe & CaRiNG SCHOOL.

Get the Whole Story

Story #1:

Mary Lou was going shopping at the grocery store for six items: milk, eggs, fruit, bread, cheese, and ice cream. On her way home, she saw her friend Sally. They agreed to go on a picnic next Wednesday at 1 p.m.

Story #1 Questions:

1) Where was Mary Lou going?
2) What was she getting there?
3) Who did she see on the way home?
4) What did they agree to do?
5) When are they going?

Story #2:

Michael went to the ballgame with his grandpa on Sunday. They ate hot dogs, pretzels, peanuts, popcorn, juice, and ice cream. The home team won, and the final score was 10 to 7. They got home at 6 p.m., just in time for supper, but they weren't hungry!

Story #2 Questions:

1) Who did Michael go to the game with?
2) What snacks did they eat?
3) Who won the game?
4) What was the final score?
5) What time did they get home?

Active Listening Practice Sheet

Speaker's Name: _____

Listener's Name: _____

Answers:

1) _____
2) _____
3) _____
4) _____
5) _____

Did the listener:

☐ sit quietly and pay attention?
☐ look at the speaker?
☐ wait until it was his or her turn to talk?
☐ remember all the information in the story?

we are a safe & caring school.

MARCH

PICTURE THIS

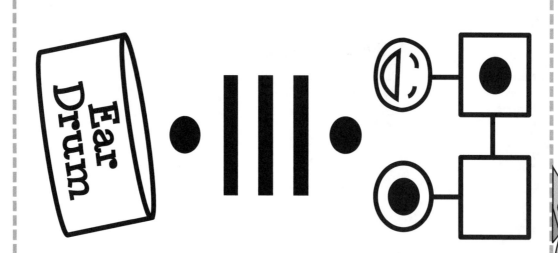

Ear Drum

Ear Drum

we are a safe & caring school.

COOL RESPONSE

The Situation	A Passive Response	An Aggressive Response	An Assertive Response
1. During lunch, a student hits you for no reason while you wait in line.			
2. Something is stolen from your class, and you are blamed; even though you didn't do it.			
3. You're watching TV and your sister or brother changes the channel without asking you.			
4. You need to call a friend, but your mom has been using the phone for a long time.			

Conflict is a part of life.

Discuss conflict with your friends and answer the following questions.

ALL ABOUT CONFLICT

What is conflict? _____

_____

_____

_____

_____

Why do people have conflicts? _____

_____

_____

_____

Conflict I've seen...	A negative response to the conflict would be...	A positive response to the conflict would be...
...at school:		
...in my neighborhood:		
...in the media:		

we are
a safe
& caring
school.

WHO'S IN CHARGE OF ME?

Sometimes when we feel upset, we might say or do things that get us into trouble.

Write about a time when something or someone upset you.

The Issue

My Actions

My Thoughts

My Choices

My Feelings

The Consequences

we are
a safe
& caring
school.

SPECIAL REPORT

You're a reporter on special assignment for the local newspaper. You need to write a **Safe & Caring Special Report** about conflict in the world. Where do you start?

First, what is conflict, what creates conflicts, and how do people resolve them?

_____
_____
_____
_____
_____
_____
_____
_____
_____
_____

Next, organize your notes. (Important!)

Story title: _____
_____

Sources of information: _____
_____
_____

Place: _____

People involved: _____
_____

What is the conflict? _____
_____

Why did it happen? _____

How could it have been prevented? ____
_____

How I feel about this conflict: _____

My idea about how to solve this conflict:
_____
_____
_____

Finally, write your story.

we aRe a saFe & CaRiNG SCHOOL.

STOP, THINK, CHOOSE CONFIDENCE CRUISE

Sail your ship to Safe & Caring Schools Island. As you and your friends cruise the uncharted waters, you will encounter challenges that build your strength. Stick to your beliefs and you'll stay on course. **Bon voyage!**

START HERE

1) You sit next to a kid who a lot of people tease.

☐ Encourage the kid and help stop the bullying.

☐ Join in and tease the kid, too.

2) Your parents expect you home right after school, but your friends want you to go with them to the mall.

☐ Communicate with your parents and your friends to work out an agreement.

☐ Take off with your friends and deal with your parents later.

3) A kid threatens to "get you" after school.

☐ Ask for help from a trusted adult.

☐ Don't say anything and take your chances.

4) A friend asks if he can copy your test.

☐ Say "no" because it's bad for both of you.

☐ Go along and help him cheat.

5) You worked hard on your school project, but your friends think it's stupid.

☐ Be proud of your work.

☐ Allow them to make you feel bad.

6) You're being bullied for speaking your mind.

☐ Be careful but be true to yourself.

☐ Care more about what *others* think than what *you* do.

7) You see someone stealing from a store.

☐ Notify the store.

☐ Ignore the situation.

SAFE & CARING SCHOOLS®

Hooray, you made it!

we are
a safe
& caring
school.

CHANGE OF ATTITUDE

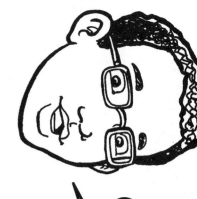

Our attitudes can be **positive** or **negative**.

When our bad attitude is not helping us, it's important to use **Stop, Think, Choose** to find a new approach.

Draw a cartoon about a time you needed to change your attitude from negative to positive.

WE ARE A SAFE & CARING SCHOOL.

CONFLICT RESOLUTION QUIZ

True or False (circle the correct answer)

1) My attitude, positive or negative, is nobody else's business. . . . . **True / False**
2) You can only get what you want from others when you interrupt . . . . **True / False**
3) Paying attention to people when they speak shows respect . . . . **True / False**
4) Conflict only happens when others do something you don't like . . . . **True / False**
5) It is important to ask questions if you do not understand . . . . **True / False**

Multiple Choice (circle the correct answer)

6) At our Safe & Caring School:
   - **a.** there are conflicts from time to time.
   - **b.** there are never any problems and everybody gets along perfectly.
   - **c.** we learn skills to prevent conflict.
   - **d.** a and c

7) Conflicts can be resolved when we:
   - **a.** stop, think, choose.
   - **b.** misunderstand how the other person feels and what he or she needs.
   - **c.** demand to resolve it our way, or no way!
   - **d.** take time to spread a few rumors.

8) When we listen carefully:
   - **a.** we hear only the part we want to hear.
   - **b.** we learn all the details of a situation or a story.
   - **c.** we don't need to stop and pay attention.
   - **d.** it is so boring.

Fill in the Blanks

9) When you speak clearly and respectfully about what you need during a conflict, you are

   being **a**_____ .

10) **C**_____ is a normal part of life. Resolving conflict in a **p**_____ way
    is a great skill to have!

Real-Life Writing

We build our confidence by practicing what we find challenging. Sometimes we feel uncomfortable when there is conflict. How can you build your confidence to resolve conflicts peacefully?

we are
a safe
& caring
SCHOOL.

SAFE & CARING SCHOOLS ®

SKILLS FOR SCHOOL. SKILLS FOR LIFE.

APRIL
The Power to Choose

- **Making Choices**
- **Consequences**
- **Peer Pressure**

Making good choices is an important and essential skill, especially for today's youth. Our students are challenged, tempted, and bullied. They have more opportunities to get into trouble than ever before. Children need to be taught to use the power of their minds in positive ways to help them make good choices every day.

MONTHLY OBJECTIVES
Students will:

- learn about the importance of making good choices
- learn what it means to be responsible for their own actions
- practice treating people with fairness and respect

TEACHING TIPS

- The key sources of anger in children are stress, frustration, feeling rejected, and feeling isolated.
- Anger is a normal human emotion.
- Teach students how to manage anger and channel its energy in productive ways.
- Children need to learn they have the power to respond to conflict in constructive ways.
- Violence is a learned behavior. With practice and positive reinforcement, students can learn to manage their anger and make better choices.

APRIL INTEGRATED ACTIVITIES

In addition to the specific lesson plans for this month, you can use these optional ideas to integrate and extend the Safe & Caring themes into your daily routines and across curricular areas.

LANGUAGE ARTS

- Write in daily or weekly journals about choices, consequences, justice, and fairness.

- Work in small groups to create 15- to 30- second public service announcements about positive choices.

- Write short stories or poems exploring feelings regarding choices and consequences.

LITERATURE

- Choose books from the library about fairness, justice, choices, and consequences. In small groups, discuss how the characters in the story treated one another and made choices.

- Have students learn about determination and the ability to problem solve and help others by reading *All for the Better: A Story of El Barrio (Stories of America)* by Nicholasa Morh. In 1933 during Puerto Rico's Great Depression, 11-year-old Evelina Lopez leaves her mother and sisters to live with an aunt in New York City. She learned her poor neighbors were too ashamed to apply for food packages, so she found a solution to the problem.

SOCIAL STUDIES

- Ask students to make a list of what they see or hear on the news (radio, television, newspaper, Internet) regarding justice. What is *injustice?*

- Ask students to research people, past or present, who have been known for their fairness.

- Have students research a historical figure whose greatest characteristics were justice and fairness. Ask them to assume the role of that individual and tell the group who they are and what they have done.

ART

- Read *The Wall* by Eve Bunting and Ronald Himler. Have students create a "wall of respect" by drawing pictures or writing stories depicting one of the character traits from this month's theme.

- Create a classroom book called, "Making Good Choices." Each student creates a page for the book that includes a drawing, poetry, short story, or facts about character traits essential to making good choices.

MUSIC

- Explore the sounds of different instruments. Have students choose the sounds they prefer. Create a musical piece to see how the sounds you choose affect the results.

MATH

- Make predictions as to how many students in class will make positive choices, show fairness, and be able to stand up for their rights in a respectful way. Write scenarios and have students respond to them. Collect data on the student responses and explain how the data supports or disproves their predictions.

Safe & Caring Vocabulary and Word Find

LEARNING OBJECTIVES

Students will:

- be introduced to vocabulary that supports understanding they have the power to choose how they respond to others
- internalize the vocabulary as they use it throughout the month and year in real-life situations

MATERIALS NEEDED

"Safe & Caring Vocabulary" (page 163) and "Safe & Caring Word Find" (page 164) activity sheets, dictionaries, pencils

LESSON PLAN

Use the vocabulary activities to introduce the concepts and common language associated with this month's theme. Throughout the month, use the words in writing, spelling, storytelling, and dealing with conflict situations.

For "Safe & Caring Schools Vocabulary," explain how to fill in the blanks to decipher the message. (You have the *power* to *choose*. When *conflicts* arise, you can make a *positive* choice or a *negative* choice. Be creative and *explore* all your *options*. Use *critical thinking* to consider how to *respond* to conflict and what the *consequences* may be. If we make *good* choices, we are *responsible* members of our safe and caring classroom *community*.)

For "Safe & Caring Word Find," discuss what the words mean after completing the page. You may want students to work in pairs to help each other.

```
C N P O W E R E W O P P
R A O V G J S E L E O Q
I U S C O S S Q G V P R
T C I C O M M U N I T Y
I C T A D C G A E T I Y
C H V P I G F L G I O T
A E E F N S R I R J N I
L A C G W T E E S L I
T R R O M N Z Y S X E I B
H A S N E R O I P P R B
I C J S S T C O L G I I
N E V I T A G E N O E D
K E F D A C Z E S R S N
I R N E I N A L I E O O
N I D R R G S D B N O P
G G H F O G A W L P H S
A C O N S E Q U E N C E
L E V I T A E R C R G R
```

I Have the Power to Choose

LEARNING OBJECTIVES

Students will:

- understand that they are responsible for their actions and the consequences of their choices
- learn that they can choose how to respond when people treat them unfairly

MATERIALS NEEDED

The book *Easing the Teasing: Helping Your Child Cope with Name-Calling, Ridicule, and Verbal Bullying* by Judy S. Freedman, "I Have the Power to Choose" activity sheet (page 165), writing and drawing tools

LESSON PLAN

READ chapter 6 of *Easing the Teasing*. Decide how you want to share this information with the students. This chapter reviews kids' options for responding to teasers, including self-talk, ignoring, I-messages, visualization, turning the tease around, humor, and when to ask for help.

> An optional text for teachers is *How to Handle Bullies, Teasers, and Other Meanies* by Kate Cohen-Posey. It provides information on what motivates people who bully and tease, including how to defend oneself from bullying, teasing, and prejudice.

DISCUSS Tell students that they have the power to choose how they respond to the way people treat them. Even if they feel angry, sad, or frustrated, they can choose what to do with their feelings. If someone chooses to use name-calling or teasing, they can choose to ignore it and walk away, use I-messages, tell the bully to stop, or ask for help.

DO the "I Have the Power to Choose" activity sheet. Brainstorm different real-life teasing situations students may have encountered. Discuss the positive and negative choices they could make in each situation and the consequences of each. Students fill in their own situation on the sheet, along with the choices and consequences they have to consider.

RELATE the activity to everyday situations the students have at school or in their communities. Have students share and compare their responses to the conflicts described on the activity sheet.

Making Positive Choices

LEARNING OBJECTIVES

Students will:

- learn that there is a direct correlation between choices and consequences
- find they can change their negative choices and experience positive consequences

MATERIALS NEEDED

The book *Elbert's Bad Word* by Audrey Wood, "Making Positive Choices" activity sheet (page 166), writing and drawing tools

LESSON PLAN

READ *Elbert's Bad Word*. A bad word spoken by Elbert creates havoc at a fashionable garden party, and Elbert gets his mouth scrubbed out with soap. The bad word, in the shape of a long-tailed furry monster, will not go away until a wizard-gardener cooks up positive words that everyone at the party applauds.

> An optional text for independent reading or teacher modeled and shared reading is *Shoeshine Girl* by Clyde Robert Bulla. Obstinate Sarah Ida learns a great deal about listening while working her summer job of shining shoes.

DISCUSS What did Elbert do that upset everyone? What were the consequences of his action? What happened when he did it again? What could he have done instead? How did Elbert solve the problem? Help students understand the direct connection between feelings, actions, and consequences.

DO the "Making Positive Choices" activity sheet. Have students put themselves into the situations and write about how they would feel in each situation, what they might choose to do, and the consequences of their choices.

RELATE the activity to daily life by asking students to share their responses with the class. If some students made negative choices, use them as teachable moments. Discuss how to change the negative choice to a positive solution and consequence. Make a list of situations and choices the kids experience.

Targeting Good Choices

LEARNING OBJECTIVES

Students will:

- recognize that stress can affect their decision-making process
- recommend positive ways to respond to stress

MATERIALS NEEDED

The book *The Handbook for Helping Kids with Anxiety and Stress* by Tip Frank and Kim Frank, "Targeting Good Choices" activity sheet (page 167), writing and drawing tools

LESSON PLAN

READ section 2 (pages 26–28, 30–42) of *The Handbook for Helping Kids with Anxiety and Stress*. This book is a collection of practical, easy-to-follow tips and activities to help kids with fears, anxieties, and phobias. The first section includes insights, hints, and suggestions for professionals and parents to help kids cope with anxiety and stress. The second section is for kids to read themselves.

> An optional text for teachers is *We Can Work It Out: Conflict Resolution for Children* by Barbara K. Polland. Polland, a professor of child development, provides strategies for helping children discuss difficult situations with adults.

DISCUSS how stress affects our ability to make appropriate choices. Make a list of stressful situations and determine the best ways to arrive at positive decisions.

DO the "Targeting Good Choices" activity sheet. Students look at a list of options people have when they feel stressed, and then decide if they are good or bad choices.

RELATE the students' choices for the situations on the activity sheet to choices they make daily. Help them practice using their creative thinking when faced with difficult choices. Validate students' feelings and encourage them to use the "Feelings Mailbox" (page 9) or talk to someone before they become overwhelmed.

Choose Wisely

LEARNING OBJECTIVES

Students will:

- be reminded that they have the power to choose
- learn about the consequences of making poor choices

MATERIALS NEEDED

The book *Pedrito's Day* by Luis Garay, "Choose Wisely" activity sheet (page 168), writing tools

LESSON PLAN

READ   *Pedrito's Day*. Pedrito shines shoes to earn money for a bicycle, but a reckless mistake forces him to make a hard decision.

DISCUSS   What did Pedrito want to do with the money he earned? What was the problem? How did Pedrito feel? What were his choices? Which choice did he make?

DO   the "Choose Wisely" activity sheet. Working in pairs, students will interview each other, asking their partners the questions on the sheet and recording their responses.

RELATE   the information collected on the activity sheets to the real world by connecting it to what the children face on a daily basis. Have partners take turns sharing the information they collected. Remind students that everyone makes poor choices sometimes. The important thing is to learn from mistakes and not repeat them the next time a similar situation comes along.

Choice Week

LEARNING OBJECTIVES

Students will:

- review how to make wise choices in difficult situations
- learn how to keep track of important choices they make on a regular basis

MATERIALS NEEDED

The book *Too Many Tamales* by Gary Soto, "Choice Week" activity sheet (page 169), writing and drawing tools

LESSON PLAN

READ   *Too Many Tamales*. Maria is making tamales, kneading the masa, and feeling grown-up. She wants a chance to wear her mother's diamond ring, so when her mother steps away, Maria tries on the ring and then gets back to her work. Only later, when the tamales are baked, does Maria remember the ring, which is no longer on her finger. She and the cousins search every tamale for the missing ring.

DISCUSS   how making choices is not always easy. Remind the students how important it is to follow through with their responsibilities. Children will always have to make choices. Have the students think of all the choices they already made today.

DO   the "Choice Week" activity sheet. Give students the sheets on Monday to record the choices they make every day for a week. Have the students record their choices in the good, bad, or so-so columns. Review the sheets on Friday.

RELATE   the decision-making activity to what students will continue to do for the rest of their lives. Sometimes students don't even realize they have made a decision. Have them share some of their easy and some of their more difficult decisions. How can we help each other to make wise choices? The power to choose is one of the most important abilities we have and learning to choose wisely is a valuable skill.

Choices & Consequences Cards

LEARNING OBJECTIVES

Students will:

- predict both positive and negative consequences of various choices
- role-play selected situations and discuss the consequences of various choices

MATERIALS NEEDED

The book *More If You Had to Choose, What Would You Do?* by Sandra McLeod Humphrey, "Choices & Consequences Cards" activity sheet (page 170), scissors, writing tools, paper

LESSON PLAN

READ   "Been There, Done That!" (pages 11–14) in *More If You Had to Choose, What Would You Do?* Andy has hard choices to make when he is paired with two students who do not want to work very hard on their assigned project.

An optional text for independent reading or teacher modeled and shared reading is *Good Grief, Third Grade* by Colleen O'Shaughnessy McKenna. Marsha vows not to get into trouble at school this year, but her good intentions change when she lies about Roger and gets him suspended.

DISCUSS Andy's choices. What do you think he will do? What are the consequences of his choices? Should he tell his teacher? What are the consequences of doing that?

DO the "Choices & Consequences Cards" activity sheet. Divide students in groups of four or five, and distribute the activity sheet to each group. Ask students to cut apart the cards and brainstorm positive solutions to each problem. Encourage them to create their own Choices & Consequences Cards (using no names). Collect all the cards. Have student groups take turns picking a card and role-playing their solution to the problem.

RELATE the activity to the students' daily lives. Ask: How are the choices we make influenced by others in positive or negative ways? Who supports you when you stand up for what you believe in and want to do the right thing?

Fair and Unfair

LEARNING OBJECTIVES

Students will:

- learn about fairness
- evaluate various situations for fairness or unfairness

MATERIALS NEEDED

The book *Bean Thirteen* by Matthew McElligott, "Fair and Unfair" activity sheet (page 171), writing tools

LESSON PLAN

READ *Bean Thirteen*. Ralph warns Flora not to pick that thirteenth bean because it's unlucky. She picks it anyway. Now, how can they make it disappear?

DISCUSS What did Ralph warn Flora about and why? Who decides what needs to be done as they divide the beans? How will they solve the problem and escape the curse of bean thirteen?

DO the "Fair and Unfair" activity sheet. Students will define *fairness*, unscramble words to finish a paragraph, and decide whether situations are fair or unfair.

RELATE the concept of fairness to what the students experience in school. Ask: Why is it sometimes fair for a child to have opportunities that his or her peers do not? What situations show this type of fairness? Why is fair not always equal? Use the dictionary and define *equality* and *equity*. How are they different? *(Equality means having the same privileges or rights where equity means justice based on fairness.)*

Helping Make School Safe & Caring

LEARNING OBJECTIVES

Students will:

- explore what it means to be accountable for their actions
- look at ways they can choose to help make their school a safe and caring place

MATERIALS NEEDED

The book *Arthur's Computer Disaster* by Marc Brown, "Helping Make School Safe & Caring" activity sheet (page 172), writing tools

LESSON PLAN

READ *Arthur's Computer Disaster*. Arthur's mother forbids him to use her computer while she is at work. However, Arthur chooses to use it anyway.

DISCUSS Did Arthur take responsibility seriously? Ask students to share examples of being responsible for their own actions. Why is it hard for people to take responsibility for the things they say and do? What can we all do to make our school a place where everyone feels safe?

DO the "Helping Make School Safe & Caring" activity sheet. Ask students to work in small groups to create a plan for handling conflict in different locations in the school.

RELATE the importance of following rules in order to keep school a safe place. Discuss the need for rules and the consequences of choosing not to follow the rules. Help students see that dealing with conflict and tough situations will always be part of their lives. School is the perfect place for them to apply new skills in dealing with friends, making good choices, and being accountable for their actions.

Good Friends Help Make Good Choices

LEARNING OBJECTIVES

Students will:

- discuss the difference between positive and negative peer pressure
- practice ways to show compassion and stand up to negative peer pressure

MATERIALS NEEDED

The book *More If You Had to Choose, What Would You Do?* by Sandra McLeod Humphrey, "Good Friends Help Make Good Choices" activity sheet (page 173), writing tools

LESSON PLAN

READ   "No Perfect 10" (pages 61–64) in *More If You Had to Choose, What Would You Do?* Clayton invites four boys to a birthday party. They want to give Clayton a hard time, so they plan to accept the invitation but not show up at the party.

An optional text for independent reading or teacher modeled and shared reading is *Nothing's Fair in the Fifth Grade* by Barthe DeClements. Elsie Edwards is on a strict diet and can only eat what her mom puts in her lunch box. She decides to steal the other students' money to buy candy and now everyone knows her as the fat thief. Jennifer learns that things are not fair for Elsie and finds a way to help.

DISCUSS   the questions at the end of the reading: Why would a person want to hurt someone else's feelings? What kind of behavior is that? Are friends like that worth keeping? How can we make a difference?

DO   the "Good Friends Help Make Good Choices" activity sheet. Students will look at different scenarios and decide what they would say and do for each. When finished, have them explain why they would or would not do something.

RELATE   the positive and negative peer pressure to everyday life and friendships. Have students make a list of real-life situations where peer pressure, choices, and consequences play a role.

Save the Earth!

LEARNING OBJECTIVES

Students will:

- learn about taking responsibility for their own actions

- explore ways they can make positive contributions to protecting the environment

MATERIALS NEEDED

The book *Earth Day—Hooray!* by Stuart J. Murphy, "Save the Earth!" activity sheet (page 174), writing tools

LESSON PLAN

READ   *Earth Day—Hooray!* Earth Day is on the way, and Ryan, Luke, and Carly have a plan. If they manage to recycle 5,000 aluminum cans, they can buy flowers for Gilroy Park.

An optional text for independent reading or teacher modeled and shared reading is *Save Our Planet: 750 Everyday Ways You Can Help Clean Up the Earth* by Diane MacEachern. The author offers tips on how to be more environmentally friendly.

DISCUSS   What are different types of responsibilities that people have (personal, legal, religious, traditions, community, environmental)? Why do we need to be responsible for these? What might happen if we choose not to help make our planet a better place? Whose responsibility is it to take care of our environment? Why?

DO   the "Save the Earth!" activity sheet. Students complete a crossword puzzle using terms related to recycling and the environment. *(Answers: 1-trash, 2-icebergs, 3-green, 4-recycle, 5-earth, 6-global, 7-ecology.)* Students may want to create their own "Save the Earth!" crossword puzzles to share with each other.

RELATE   what the students learned about recycling and responsibility to making positive contributions in their communities. Ask students to think of what they can do to help with our environment. Possible next steps might be to write letters to government officials, educate others, create and perform a play about saving our planet, start a recycling program at school, or study what other kids do around the world to save the planet.

The Power to Choose Quiz

To assess student progress, use the quiz on page 175. *(Answers: 1-F, 2-T, 3-T, 4-F, 5-T, 6-c, 7-c, 8-b, 9-power, choices, 10-consequences)*

Safe & Caring Vocabulary

Fill in the blanks below with the correct words from the list.

community   explore   options
choose   positive   responsible
good   critical thinking   consequences
conflicts   power   respond
                    negative

You have the _ _ _ _ _ to _ _ _ _ _ _.

When _ _ _ _ _ _ _ _ _ arise, you can make

a _ _ _ _ _ _ _ _ choice or a _ _ _ _ _ _ _ _ choice.

Be creative and _ _ _ _ _ _ _ all your _ _ _ _ _ _ _.

Use _ _ _ _ _ _ _ _ _ _ _ _ _ _ _ _ to consider

how to _ _ _ _ _ _ _ to conflict and what

the _ _ _ _ _ _ _ _ _ _ _ _ may be. If we make _ _ _ _

choices, we are _ _ _ _ _ _ _ _ _ _ _ _ members

of our safe and caring classroom _ _ _ _ _ _ _ _ _.

Define the word **option**. _____

_____

_____

When in conflict, why should we consider the consequences
of our actions? _____

_____

_____

we are
a safe
& caring
SCHOOL.

Safe & Caring WORD FIND

Find and circle the words listed at the bottom of the page.

(Hint: Answers can run forward, backward, up, down, or diagonally.)

C	N	P	O	W	E	R	E	W	O	P	P	P
R	A	O	V	G	J	S	E	L	E	O	Q	
I	U	S	C	O	S	S	Q	G	V	P	R	
T	C	I	C	O	M	M	U	N	I	T	Y	
I	C	T	A	D	C	G	A	E	T	I	Y	
C	C	I	P	I	G	F	L	G	I	O	T	
A	H	V	L	N	S	R	I	R	J	N	I	
L	A	E	C	F	G	W	T	E	E	S	L	
T	R	R	O	M	N	Z	Y	S	X	E	I	
H	A	S	N	E	R	O	I	P	P	R	B	
I	C	J	S	S	T	I	C	O	L	G	I	
N	E	V	I	T	A	G	E	N	O	E	D	
K	E	F	D	A	C	Z	E	S	R	S	N	
I	R	N	E	I	N	A	L	I	E	O	O	
N	I	D	R	R	G	S	D	B	N	O	P	
G	G	H	F	O	G	A	W	L	P	H	S	
A	C	O	N	S	E	Q	U	E	N	C	E	
L	E	V	I	T	A	E	R	C	R	G	R	

GOOD   COMMUNITY   RESPOND

CONFLICT   RESPONSIBLE   NEGATIVE

EXPLORE   CONSEQUENCE   OPTIONS

CHOOSE   POSITIVE   CRITICAL THINKING

POWER   CREATIVE   CONSIDER

we are
a safe
& caring
school.

I Have The POWER TO CHOOSE

Good Choice

Consequence

APRIL

The Situation

Choice Machine

we are a safe & caring school.

Bad Choice

Consequence

Making Positive Choices

The Situation	How would I feel?	What would I choose to do?	What might happen?
Someone called you names.			
Someone put you down.			
Someone got into your desk without your permission.			
You were being pushed around.			
You were being left out.			
Someone spread rumors about you.			
You made a mistake in class, and everyone laughed.			
You weren't invited to a birthday party.			
You were picked last for a team.			
No one picked you for their project partner.			
You asked someone to share, and they turned you down.			

WE ARE
A SAFE
& CARING
SCHOOL.

TARGETING GOOD CHOICES

Sometimes when we feel stressed, we have a hard time making good choices.

Look at the list of options you have when you feel worried, frustrated, sad, or afraid. Draw a line to target a good choice ⊕ or a bad choice ⊖.

- sleep all day
- listen to music
- talk to someone you trust
- skip school
- draw a picture or cartoon
- eat too much
- read a book
- help a friend
- take a walk or run
- ignore your homework
- write in a journal
- watch TV all day
- go for a bike ride
- refuse to leave your room
- ask for help

Select one ⊕ choice from above and explain why it's ⊕ .

_____

_____

_____

Select one ⊖ choice from above and explain why it's ⊖ .

_____

_____

_____

we are
a safe
& caring
school.

CHOOSE WISELY

Work with a partner to interview each other and answer the following questions.

Describe a poor choice you once made.

_____
_____
_____
_____
_____
_____

What were the consequences of your choice?

_____
_____
_____
_____
_____
_____

What were your other options? _____

_____
_____
_____
_____
_____

What did you learn from making the choice you did? _____

_____
_____
_____
_____
_____

we aRe
a safe
& CaRiNG
SCHOOL.

Being **accountable** means taking responsibility for your choices. List the important choices you made this week.

CHOICE WEEK

 Good choices you made

 Bad choices you made

 So-so choices you made

Monday

Tuesday

Wednesday

Thursday

Friday

CHOICES & CONSEQUENCES CARDS

You bump into someone by accident. You apologize, but he is still angry.

You're blamed for something you didn't do.

Your favorite TV show is starting, but your mom says you have to clean your room.

A friend borrows your skateboard and breaks it.

You are being bullied every time your teacher looks the other way.

Your friends ask you to choose between them.

You want to go riding with your friends, but you have a big test tomorrow.

The new kid in class is being excluded by your friends, and you stick up for her.

You are being pressured to do something you know is wrong.

If someone calls you a bad name, you...

You're behind on your English report, and your sister won't get off the computer when you need it.

Being in a play looks like fun, but your friends say you're a sissy for wanting to do it.

we are a safe & caring school.

Fairness means treating people justly.

Unscramble the words below and write them in the correct spaces.

FAiR & UNFAiR

Fair doesn't always mean equal. Describe what fairness means to you.

_____

_____

_____

_____

_____

_____

_____

I have seen things that are _ _ _ _ _ _ at _ _ _ _, at
                            n a i f u r   h o e m

_ _ _ _ _ _, and in the _ _ _ _ _. I have heard that _ _ _ _ is not
o l s c h o   d i m a e   f e l i

always _ _ _ _, but I can _ _ _ _ _ _ to be a fair person.
       i r a f   s h o c o e

Read each sentence below and decide if it's fair or unfair, and then explain.

Situation	Fair	Unfair	Explain your choices
You're blamed for something you did not do.			
Your friends don't want to hang out with you anymore.			
You're being bullied, and some people say it's your fault.			
Sally, who has crutches, gets to go first in line.			

we are a safe & caring school.

SAFE & CARING
HELPING MAKE SCHOOL

If everyone does their part, school can be a great place to be!

How can you be helpful in your school?

Brainstorm ways you and your friends can help make your school a safe and caring place.

Names of Group Members	Location	Ways I Can Help
	In the classroom	
	In your school hallways	
	In school common areas	
	In the school cafeteria	
	In school bathrooms	
	On the playground	
	In the school computer room	
	In the library	
	Other?	

WE ARE A SAFE & CARING SCHOOL.

APRIL

GOOD FRIENDS HELP MAKE GOOD CHOICES

What would you do in the situations below? What would you say to your friends?

Do good friends try to get you into trouble?

No! Good friends help me stay out of trouble.

Situation	Would you do it?	What do you say?
Your friends want you to play a mean trick on the new kid in school.		
Your friend thinks you should let your parents know before going to his house after school.		
Your friend thinks it would be funny to sneak inside your school during recess.		
Your friend doesn't like a certain girl and wants you to exclude her from your group.		
Your friend was chosen to be an Ambassador of Peace and would like you to be one, too.		

we are a safe & caring school.

SAVE THE EARTH!

1. People throw away too much
2. These are shrinking
3. The color of environmentally safe products
4. To collect trash to be used again
5. The planet where we live
6. The type of warming we are concerned about
7. Science dealing with the environment

We are
a safe
& caring
school.

THE POWER TO CHOOSE QUIZ

True or False (circle the correct answer)

1) We cannot tell what the consequences of our choices may be
   so why even think about them . . . . **True / False**

2) If we are stressed it can be harder to make good choices . . . . **True / False**

3) It is smart to explore all your options when you are making choices. . . . . **True / False**

4) Blaming someone else instead of taking responsibility for what we do
   is a positive choice . . . . **True / False**

5) We can choose to be fair, even though life can sometimes be unfair. . . . . **True / False**

Multiple Choice (circle the correct answer)

6) At our Safe & Caring School:
   - **a.** what we choose to do is not important.
   - **b.** it is best to let others make choices for us.
   - **c.** our classroom community is a safe place to think about our options.
   - **d.** we don't have anything to choose, everything is already decided for us.

7) When we are stressed-out:
   - **a.** we cannot get help from people we know and trust.
   - **b.** it is okay to be a bully.
   - **c.** we can stop, think, choose a positive way to help us feel better.
   - **d.** a and c.

8) Good friends help us:
   - **a.** get into trouble.
   - **b.** make sure to get permission when needed.
   - **c.** break rules in sneaky ways.
   - **d.** join the cool kids by finding something mean to do to prove how fun you are.

Fill in the Blanks

9) You have the **p**_____to make good **c**_____.

10) While thinking about the choices we can make, it is important to think about the

    c_____of those choices.

Real-Life Writing

Caring enough to make wise choices is good for you and your Safe & Caring School community.
Your friends make poor choices sometimes and tell you that you care too much about what you choose
to do. What can you tell them about the importance of choosing wisely?

we are a safe & caring school.

SAFE & CARING SCHOOLS ®

SKILLS FOR SCHOOL. SKILLS FOR LIFE.

MAY
Follow Your Dreams

- **Goal Setting**
- **Perseverance**
- **Celebration of Self**

In order for children to reach for their dreams, they need to recognize their strengths and abilities. They deserve our ongoing support and constant reminders that we believe in them.

MONTHLY OBJECTIVES
Students will:

- understand the importance of facing challenges with persistence and positive attitudes
- realize that having dreams and hopes helps them plan for the future
- learn how to set goals and plan the steps to achieve them
- self-evaluate and celebrate their growth and successes during the year

TEACHING TIPS

- Help children connect new learning to real-life experiences.
- Develop the power of young minds by stirring their imagination through creative play, thinking, and writing.
- Improve children's well-being by letting them know you believe in them.
- Recognize small accomplishments on a daily basis. Success brings more success.

In addition to the specific lesson plans for this month, you can use these optional ideas to integrate and extend the Safe & Caring themes into your daily routines and across curricular areas.

LANGUAGE ARTS

- Have students write an essay, short story, or poem about something they want to do better and what they think they can do to make it happen.
- Ask students to write short stories about their dreams for the future. Collect the stories and read a few each day without sharing the name of the students. This helps students realize that everyone has hopes and dreams.

LITERATURE

- Have students visit the library and look for books dealing with motivation, self-discipline, and perseverance (for example: *Cinder Edna* by Ellen Jackson or *The Lotus Seed* by Sherry Garland).

SOCIAL STUDIES

- Discuss people who succeeded in life because they followed their dreams.
- Research how Cinco de Mayo became a special day of celebration. Use *Viva Mexico! The Story of Benito Juarez; Cinco de Mayo: Stories of America; or Celebrate! It's Cinco de Mayo / Celebremos Es El Cinco de Mayo* by Janice Levy as resources.
- Invite special guests (parents, community members, school staff) to share information about their jobs.
- Organize "Career Day" and help students dress up to represent people in different jobs.
- Watch the movie *Homeward Bound* and ask students to write about an example they saw in the movie that showed perseverance.

ART

- Create a classroom book called "Following Your Dreams." Have students draw pictures and write about their dreams.
- Decorate a shoebox together as a class and call it, "I know I can." Students record on paper the challenges they face and place them in the box.
- Create posters that celebrate growing up and decorate the hallways with them.

MUSIC

- Have students create a musical representation of their lives through sounds, melodies, lyrics, or pieces of existing songs. Have them add a finale to the musical piece that represents what they think their lives will be like if they follow their dreams.

MATH

- Use a survey to find out the career interests of students. Determine the percentages of how many students like each type of career.
- Compare the number of girls and boys who like certain careers.
- Create a timeline to show how long it might take to pursue each career.
- Create a graph that shows the many talents of your students.

Safe & Caring Vocabulary and Word Find

LEARNING OBJECTIVES

Students will:

- be introduced to vocabulary that supports learning how to follow their dreams
- internalize the vocabulary as they use it throughout the month and year in real-life situations

MATERIALS NEEDED

"Safe & Caring Vocabulary" (page 183) and "Safe & Caring Word Find" (page 184) activity pages, dictionaries, pencils

LESSON PLAN

Use the vocabulary activities to introduce the concepts and common language associated with this month's theme. Throughout the month, use the words in writing, spelling, storytelling, and dealing with conflict situations.

For "Safe & Caring Schools Vocabulary," explain how to unscramble the words to decipher the message. (Following your _hopes_ and _dreams_ can be both _fun_ and a _challenge_. It takes _creativity_ and _discipline_ to achieve your _goals_. When you face a big challenge, stay _motivated_, keep a positive _attitude_, and have _confidence_ in your _talents_. Work _smart_, keep going, and _celebrate_ each _step_ you take on the path to _success_.)

For "Safe & Caring Word Find," discuss what the words mean after completing the page. You may want students to work in pairs to help each other.

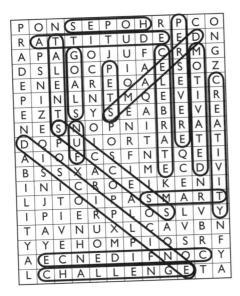

Heroes

LEARNING OBJECTIVES

Students will:

- identify their heroes
- recognize their own strengths and talents

MATERIALS NEEDED

The book _The Black Snowman_ by Phil Mendez, "Heroes" activity sheet (page 185), writing and drawing tools

LESSON PLAN

READ   _The Black Snowman_. A young boy discovers his heritage as well as his own self-worth with the help of a magical snowman made from city slush.

DISCUSS   Why was the young boy upset? What was the problem? Who helped him out? What did he learn from the snowman? What is a _hero?_ Who can be a hero? Who is a positive influence in your life? Talk about family, friends, or historical figures the students look up to.

_DO_   the "Heroes" activity sheet. Students will draw a picture of someone they believe is a hero. Then they look at themselves and recognize their own strengths or the strengths they would like to develop.

RELATE   the characteristics of heroes to people the students know. Recognize and celebrate their strengths and talents. Discuss the fact that some people idolize the wrong kind of "hero." Who might those people be and why would someone think of them as heroes?

Lots to Celebrate

LEARNING OBJECTIVES

Students will:

- make the connection between the skills they learn at school and reaching their goals in life
- learn to recognize and celebrate accomplishments

MATERIALS NEEDED

The book _Dancing in the Wings_ by Debbie Allen, "Lots to Celebrate!" activity sheet (page 186), writing and drawing tools

LESSON PLAN

READ   _Dancing in the Wings_. Sassy tries out for a summer dance festival even though the other girls taunt her and tell her that she is much too tall.

DISCUSS   What was Sassy's big dream? What did the other girls say to her? How did Sassy feel? What did she choose to do to make her dream come true? Explain that we often need to work hard to reach our dreams. When things get tough, we can't give up. Explain to students that learning new skills creates new possibilities in our lives. At school we learn skills and knowledge that help us accomplish our goals.

DO   the "Lots to Celebrate!" activity sheet. Students will respond to what we learn in school and why it is important.

RELATE   the importance of having faith in ourselves to success in all parts of our lives. Ask: What is pride? When do you feel proud? Discuss the sense of pride that we have when we accomplish our goals.

Job Charades

LEARNING OBJECTIVES

Students will:

- be introduced to different careers in their community
- discuss what they would like to be when they grow up

MATERIALS NEEDED

The book *When I Grow Up* by Marcy Brown and Dennis Haley, "Job Charades" template (page 187), scissors

LESSON PLAN

READ   *When I Grow Up*. This book has full-color photographs of people holding different jobs.

> An optional text for independent reading or teacher modeled and shared reading is *Yang the Youngest and His Terrible Ear* by Lensey Namioka. A young boy tries to play music in a family recital, but he would rather be on the baseball field.

DISCUSS   the kinds of jobs people have at school, in the neighborhood, or at home. Identify the responsibilities of each job.

DO   the "Job Charades" activity. Prepare ahead of time by cutting the activity sheet apart into the various job cards. Place the job cards into a bag. Have a student pull a card from the bag and act out the job without talking. Others will guess what job the student is demonstrating.

RELATE   the many career choices to the opportunities the students have when they grow up. Ask: Which careers from the game would you like to explore further? What new jobs have been created since you were born? Do you think there might be entirely new careers by the time you are adults?

Who Do You Call?

LEARNING OBJECTIVES

Students will:

- discover they may have talents and interests now that could direct their career choices
- learn where to get assistance if they need help in real-life situations

MATERIALS NEEDED

The book *Boy, Can He Dance!* by Eileen Spinelli, "Who Do You Call?" activity sheet (page 188), writing tools

LESSON PLAN

READ   *Boy, Can He Dance!* A young boy wants to be a professional dancer, but his father wants him to be a chef.

DISCUSS   What is the boy's dream? What does his father want him to be when he grows up? How does the boy feel about that? What changes his father's mind at the end of the story?

DO   the "Who Do You Call?" activity sheet. Students will identity the person or profession that would supply the named services. As an extension to this activity, invite parents and people from the neighborhood to talk with the class about their jobs.

RELATE   what the class learned about striving for their own goals to achieve success in all aspects of life. Have a discussion about the different careers children might like when they grow up. Point out how many different jobs they have to choose from. Encourage students that following their dreams means always trying to be the best they can be.

Dream Steps

LEARNING OBJECTIVES

Students will:

- learn to identify a goal
- create a plan to attain their goal

MATERIALS NEEDED

The book *Ziggy's Blue Ribbon Day* by Claudia Mills, "Dream Steps" activity sheet (page 189), writing and drawing tools

LESSON PLAN

READ   *Ziggy's Blue Ribbon Day*. Ziggy doesn't excel on the playing field, but he has many other talents.

An optional text for independent reading or teacher modeled and shared reading is *Rosie Swanson: Fourth-Grade Geek for President* by Barbara Park. Determined to become class president, unpopular Rosie Swanson launches a campaign with her friends.

DISCUSS   What where Ziggy's talents? How did he show those talents? What talents do you have?

DO   the "Dream Steps" activity sheet. Students can use the sheet to plan three steps that will help them accomplish one of their goals.

RELATE   this lesson to times when students felt like giving up. Review the "Dream Steps" sheets to reinforce the idea that students can divide a goal into smaller steps so it can be accomplished.

When I Grow Up, My Dream Is to Be

LEARNING OBJECTIVES

Students will:

- share what their dream job may be when they grow up
- learn that it takes motivation and perseverance to accomplish something

MATERIALS NEEDED

The book *Someday* by Eileen Spinelli, "When I Grow Up, My Dream Is to Be" activity sheet (page 190), writing and drawing tools

LESSON PLAN

READ   *Someday*. Goldie dreams of a busy future as an archaeologist, an animal scientist, an Olympic gymnast, and more.

An optional text for teacher shared reading is *The Dream Quilt* by Amy Zerner and Jessie Spicerzerner. Alex spends a week in the guest room at his great-aunt's house. Every night the "magic" quilt on his bed leads him into a different dream.

DISCUSS   What were some of the things Goldie wanted to do when she grew up? How many different jobs did she dream about? Would you like to explore any of the jobs Goldie dreamed about?

DO   the "When I Grow Up, My Dream Is to Be" activity sheet. Students will draw and write about a job they would like when they grow up.

RELATE   this lesson about having high aspirations to the students' daily lives. Have students volunteer to share their dreams with the class. Encourage them to look at all possibilities and future opportunities as they explore different careers. Discuss how they can use their skills and talents to reach for their dreams. You may want to conclude by creating a class dream quilt using student artwork.

Perseverance

LEARNING OBJECTIVES

Students will:

- use their own words to define perseverance
- practice giving affirmations to their peers who make strong efforts to accomplish goals

MATERIALS NEEDED

The book *America's Champion Swimmer: Gertrude Ederle* by David A. Adler, "Perseverance" activity sheet (page 191), writing tools

LESSON PLAN

READ   *America's Champion Swimmer: Gertrude Ederle*. This picture-book biography covers the life of Gertrude Ederle, a world record–breaking, long-distance swimmer.

DISCUSS   What were Gertrude's biggest challenges? What did she have to do to be able to compete with men? What kept her from giving up when things got tough?

DO the "Perseverance" activity sheet. Have students write their definition of *perseverance*, then think of a friend who demonstrates perseverance, and write a tribute to that person. You may want to extend this activity by having students research people who showed perseverance and then write a short report explaining what they did.

RELATE perseverance to life at school or home. Ask: How does your perseverance affect the outcomes of what you do at school or at home? Have you ever worked on something that was too hard and you just wanted to give up? What did you do in that situation? Who can you go to for help when you feel frustrated or stuck? Why is it important to keep trying even when things get tough?

Safe, Caring, & Inspired

LEARNING OBJECTIVES

Students will:

- discuss role models and how they can have a positive impact on their lives
- identify people who inspire them

MATERIALS NEEDED

The book *Dare to Dream! 25 Extraordinary Lives* by Sandra McLeod Humphrey, "Safe, Caring, & Inspired" activity sheet (page 192), writing tools

LESSON PLAN

READ selections from *Dare to Dream! 25 Extraordinary Lives*. This book is a collection of biographical sketches of people who became successful in the face of adversity. They are great candidates to become heroes for young people.

DISCUSS What did the individuals have in common? What were some of the roadblocks to their success? What helped them go on? Who inspired or directed them?

DO the "Safe, Caring, & Inspired" activity sheet. Have students define *inspiration* and *role model*. Then have each student name a person he or she considers to be a role model and answer questions about that person.

RELATE inspiration, heroes, and role models to the students' lives. Ask: Do you know any superheroes? How are you affected by role models? What do role models do that make you want to do the same? Are role models always positive?

Safe & Caring You

LEARNING OBJECTIVES

Students will:

- learn about young, inspiring leaders who made positive contributions to the world
- share ways they can personally contribute to help create a safer world

MATERIALS NEEDED

The book *We Were There, Too! Young People in U.S. History* by Phillip M. Hoose, "Safe & Caring You" activity sheet (page 193), writing and drawing tools

LESSON PLAN

READ excerpts from *We Were There, Too! Young People in U.S. History*. This book tells the stories of young people (heroes) who made big impacts in the United States.

DISCUSS how the young people used courage to help those around them. Who inspired them to care about making a difference? What surprised you or impressed you the most?

DO the "Safe & Caring You" activity sheet. Students will draw situations where they can help make a difference.

RELATE inspiration and making a difference to youth who make positive contributions wherever they are. If you could change one thing to make the world a better place, what would that be? What can you do to make a positive contribution at home or at school?

Mobilize Your Dreams

LEARNING OBJECTIVES

Students will:

- learn how to set a goal and take steps to reach that goal
- explore the concept of perseverance

MATERIALS NEEDED

The book *Zora Hurston and the Chinaberry Tree* by William Miller, writing and drawing tools, scissors, magazines, wire or coat hangers, string, construction paper, hole punch, glue

LESSON PLAN

READ   *Zora Hurston and the Chinaberry Tree.* A young girl has many dreams and learns many things as she listens to her neighbors' stories from the top of a chinaberry tree.

DISCUSS   What were Zora's dreams? What did she see from the top of the chinaberry tree? What did she learn from the stories the villagers told?

DO   Make dream mobiles to support goal setting and perseverance. Have students write their dreams on pieces of construction paper and cut out pictures in magazines that depict some aspect of the dreams. Glue the pictures to colored paper and hang them along with the dream statements, using wire or a coat hanger to create a mobile.

RELATE   goal setting to students' lives. Ask: What happens if you don't set goals? Who is responsible for your future? Have students take turns talking about their dream mobiles with the class. Hang the mobiles around the classroom. When parents visit the classroom, invite them to find their children's mobiles.

Safe & Caring End-of-Year Celebration

LEARNING OBJECTIVES
Students will:

- identify their accomplishments and growth during the school year
- celebrate their accomplishments

MATERIALS NEEDED
The book *Leonardo, Beautiful Dreamer* by Robert Byrd, "Safe & Caring End-of-Year Celebration" activity sheet (page 194), writing tools

LESSON PLAN

READ   *Leonardo, Beautiful Dreamer.* This book outlines Leonardo da Vinci's life, work, and dreams, and it gives tribute to a man whose curiosity and artistic imagination amazed the world.

DISCUSS   Who is Leonardo da Vinci? What do you know about him? What are Leonardo's greatest accomplishments? How did Leonardo use his imagination and creativity?

DO   the "Safe & Caring End-of-Year Celebration" activity sheet. Ask students to record memorable moments from the school year by responding to the prompts on the sheet.

RELATE   what the students accomplished during the school year to their social and emotional growth. Ask: What are some of your favorite accomplishments? How do you define success? Tell students that all success, no matter how small it may seem, deserves a celebration. Allow time to talk about moving forward, growing up, changing, and the amazing things they can look forward to in the next year.

Follow Your Dreams Quiz

To assess student progress, use the quiz on page 195. *(Answers: 1-F, 2-T, 3-F, 4-T, 5-T, 6-d, 7-a, 8-d, 9-share, goals, 10-school)*

Safe & Caring Vocabulary

Fill in the blanks by unscrambling the words.

Following your _ _ _ _ _ and _ _ _ _ _ _ can
          esoph   admers

be both _ _ _ and a _ _ _ _ _ _ _ _ _ . It takes
        nuf   lechelang

_ _ _ _ _ _ _ _ _ and _ _ _ _ _ _ _ _ _ to achieve
vitcrateiy   splidicein

your _ _ _ _ _. When you face a big challenge,
     agslo

stay _ _ _ _ _ _ _ _ _, keep a positive _ _ _ _ _ _ _ _,
     vetadomit   tuttadie

and have _ _ _ _ _ _ _ _ _ _ in your _ _ _ _ _ _ _.
         neefincocd   estlant

Work _ _ _ _ _, keep going, and _ _ _ _ _ _ _ _ _ each
     rastm   elebracet

_ _ _ _ you take on the path to _ _ _ _ _ _ _.
tesp   scusecs

Define the word **motivation**. _____

_____

_____

Write a sentence using the words **persevere** and
celebration. _____

_____

_____

we are
a safe
& caring
school.

SAFE & CARING WORD FIND

Find and circle the words listed at the bottom of the page.
(Hint: Answers can run forward, backward, up, down, or diagonally.)

P	O	N	S	E	P	O	H	R	P	C	O
R	A	T	T	I	T	U	D	E	E	D	N
A	P	A	G	O	J	U	F	C	R	M	G
D	S	L	O	C	P	I	A	E	S	O	Z
E	N	E	A	R	E	O	A	L	E	T	C
P	I	N	L	N	T	M	Q	E	V	I	R
E	Z	T	S	Y	S	E	A	B	E	V	E
N	E	S	N	O	P	N	I	R	R	A	A
D	Q	P	U	I	O	R	T	A	E	T	T
A	I	O	F	C	S	F	N	T	Q	E	I
B	S	S	X	A	C	I	M	E	C	D	V
I	N	I	C	R	O	E	J	K	E	N	I
L	J	T	O	I	P	A	S	M	A	R	T
I	P	I	E	R	P	L	O	S	L	V	Y
T	A	V	N	U	X	L	C	A	V	B	N
Y	Y	E	H	O	M	P	I	Q	S	R	F
A	E	C	N	E	D	I	F	N	O	C	Y
L	C	H	A	L	L	E	N	G	E	T	A

FUN	DREAMS	CELEBRATE
HOPES	PERSEVERE	SUCCESS
SMART	STEP	DISCIPLINE
ATTITUDE	CONFIDENCE	CREATIVITY
GOALS	MOTIVATED	
CHALLENGE	TALENTS	

we are
a safe
& caring
school.

HEROES

Heroes are people with character and skills we think are cool.

People we admire help us think about the good things we want to do!

Totally Cool Person

Draw

_____
Name of Cool Person

We all have ideas and skills to share. Check which skills you have, and which skills you'd *like to have*. Then add two of your own.

My Strengths

Making music . . . . ☐ Have. . . . . ☐ Would like to have

Playing sports . . . . ☐ Have. . . . . ☐ Would like to have

Coloring and drawing . . . . ☐ Have. . . . . ☐ Would like to have

Good listener and friend. . . . . ☐ Have. . . . . ☐ Would like to have

Cooking . . . . ☐ Have. . . . . ☐ Would like to have

_____ ☐ Have. . . . . ☐ Would like to have
Other

_____ ☐ Have. . . . . ☐ Would like to have
Other

we aRe a saFe & CaRiNG SCHOOL.

LOTS TO CELEBRATE

Knowing how to read is important. Why? _____

_____

_____

Math and science can help me understand a lot about how the world works. Why?_____

_____

_____

Writing my thoughts down can help me explore my dreams. Why?

_____

_____

Having a safe and caring school gives me a chance to build my skills and discover cool things I want to try. Why? _____

_____

_____

_____

Draw or write two things you've done that make you proud.

we are
a safe
& caring
SCHOOL.

JOB CHARADES

Pilot	Teacher	Athlete
Firefighter	Photographer	Doctor
Dentist	Painter	Barber
Ambulance Driver	Musician	Secretary
Train Engineer	Police Officer	Baker
Artist	Judge	Plumber
Music Conductor	Singer	Fashion Model
Bus Driver	Carpenter	Jockey
Dancer	Scientist	Movie Director
Farmer	Clown	TV Announcer
Chef	Nurse	Engineer

we are
a safe
& caring
school.

MAY

WHO DO YOU CALL?

The family car is making strange noises. _____

Your hair is getting too long. _____

The refrigerator breaks down. _____

Water is leaking in the kitchen. _____

The electricity goes off. _____

Your dog needs medicine. _____

Your computer has a problem. _____

Your family needs to borrow money
to buy a new house or car. _____

Your family wants to change
the color of your room. _____

Your tooth is aching. _____

You have stomach pain. _____

There is a medical emergency. _____

**we are
a safe
& caring
school.**

DReam STeps

Step 4

People Who Can Help

Step 3

we are a safe & caring school.

Things I Need

Step 2

Step 1

WHEN I GROW UP MY DREAM IS TO BE...

we are
a safe
& caring
school.

PERSEVERANCE

If you could give a prize to a friend who never gives up no matter how hard things get, who would you choose?

Create a "Great Job!" card for this person.

Someone who never gives up is:

_____
Name

You rock because:

To me, **perseverance** means: _____

_____

_____

_____

_____

_____

_____

we are
a safe
& caring
school.

MAY

SAFE, CARING, & INSPIRED

Do you know someone who **inspires** you? Someone who is a positive **role model**?

Define **motivation**. _____

_____

Define **role model**. _____

_____

Use them both in a sentence. _____

_____

_____

Who is a role model that you like, and why?

How does she or he affect the way you think?

How does she or he affect the way you feel?

What qualities do you wish you shared with your role model?

Real World Imagine getting advice from your role model. How would he or she help make your school a safe and caring place?

we are a safe & caring school.

Safe & Caring You

Draw pictures of yourself helping to make your home, school, neighborhood, and world safe and caring places.

There's only one **you!**

we are a safe & caring school.

School	World

Home	Neighborhood

MAY

Safe & Caring
End-of-Year Celebration

List your favorite things from school this year to share with your friends and family.

What were
your favorite
things at school
this year?

New words I learned

Books I read

My favorite field trips

My teammates

Great songs I learned

Fun things I studied

Favorite projects I worked on

New friends I made

WE ARE
A SAFE
& CARING
SCHOOL.

FOLLOW YOUR DREAMS QUIZ

True or False (circle the correct answer)

1) Once we set a goal, most of the work is done . . . .**True / False**

2) With a positive attitude we can stay motivated . . . .**True / False**

3) Making and achieving goals is too hard, so why bother? . . . .**True / False**

4) Dreams give us something to work for . . . .**True / False**

5) When we stick to a task, we can be proud of our perseverance as well as the result . . . .**True / False**

Multiple Choice (circle the correct answer)

6) At our Safe & Caring School:
   - **a.** we have lots to celebrate.
   - **b.** we join our classmates to make and achieve goals.
   - **c.** we ask for help when we need it so we don't give up.
   - **d.** all of the above

7) Role models:
   - **a.** are people we look up to and who help us try new challenges.
   - **b.** never make mistakes because they are perfect in every way.
   - **c.** make us feel bad because they are so much better than we are.
   - **d.** all of the above

8) I can help make the world a Safe & Caring place when I:
   - **a.** encourage others to do the right thing.
   - **b.** help others feel better when things don't turn out very well.
   - **c.** celebrate the successes of others.
   - **d.** all of the above

Fill in the Blanks

9) We all have skills we can **s**_____with others to help achieve **g**_____.

10) Our Safe & Caring **s**_____is a place where we can set new goals.

Real-Life Writing

It's important to have goals. We can't do everything, but it is good to keep trying. Your friend has tried hard to do something and it just didn't work out. She or he is discouraged. What can you say to encourage your friend?

RECOMMENDED RESOURCES

BOOKS

All Kids Are Our Kids: What Communities Must Do to Raise Caring and Responsible Children and Adolescents by Peter L. Benson (San Francisco: Jossey-Bass, 1997). Challenges all community members to take responsibility for the development and well-being of the community's children. Emphasizes asset building.

Building Academic Success on Social and Emotional Learning: What Does the Research Say? edited by Joseph E. Zins, Roger P. Weissberg, Margaret C. Wang, and Herbert J. Walberg (New York: Teachers College Press, 2004). Explains the science and research supporting the integration of social and emotional learning (SEL) into school curriculum.

The Bully Free Classroom by Allan L. Beane (Minneapolis: Free Spirit Publishing, 2004). More than 100 bullying prevention and intervention strategies for teachers of grades K–8.

Caring Classrooms/Intelligent Schools: The Social Emotional Education of Young Children edited by Jonathan Cohen (New York: Teachers College Press, 2001). Experts provide tips and strategies for integrating SEL into the school day.

Educating Minds and Hearts: Social Emotional Learning and the Passage into Adolescence edited by Jonathan Cohen (New York: Teachers College Press, 1999). Explains the theory and science supporting SEL and provides overviews of successful SEL programs across the nation.

Emotional Intelligence: Why It Can Matter More than I.Q. by Daniel P. Goleman (New York: Bantam Books, 2006). Explains how and why emotional intelligence is a key factor in determining career success, relationship satisfaction, overall well-being, and more.

Emotionally Intelligent Parenting: How to Raise a Self-Disciplined, Responsible, Socially Skilled Child by Maurice J. Elias, Steve E. Tobias, and Brian S. Friedlander (New York: Harmony Books, 1997). Contains advice and practical strategies on how to foster emotional intelligence in children.

Growing Good Kids: 28 Activities to Enhance Self-Awareness, Compassion, and Leadership by Deb Delisle and Jim Delisle (Minneapolis: Free Spirit Publishing, 1996). Classroom-tested activities for grades 3–8 that build students' skills in problem solving, decision making, cooperative learning, and more.

Higher Expectations: Promoting Social Emotional Learning and Academic Achievement in Your School by Raymond J. Pasi (New York: Teachers College Press, 2001). Helpful advice on how to design and implement a successful SEL program in your classroom, school, and school district.

Multiple Intelligences: The Theory in Practice by Howard Gardner (New York: Basic Books, 1993). Practical applications of multiple intelligence theory for educators.

Promoting Social and Emotional Learning: Guidelines for Educators by Maurice J. Elias (Alexandria, VA: Association for Supervision and Curriculum Development, 1997). Advice on how to advocate for, develop, implement, and evaluate schoolwide SEL programs.

Raising a Thinking Child: Help Your Child to Resolve Everyday Conflicts and Get Along with Others by Myrna B. Shure with Theresa Foy DiGeronimo (New York: Henry Holt, 1994). Tips for helping kids become independent thinkers with the self-esteem, self-confidence, and problem-solving skills to handle challenges throughout life.

Raising a Thinking Preteen: The "I Can Problem Solve" Program for 8- to 12-Year-Olds by Myrna B. Shure with Roberta Israeloff (New York: Henry Holt: 2000). Advice for fostering independent thinking, problem-solving skills, and self-confidence in tweens.

Resiliency: What We Have Learned by Bonnie Benard (San Francisco: WestEd, 2004). Summarizes ten years of research on resiliency development in children and offers suggestions on how to incorporate and apply the research in everyday life.

What Kids Need to Succeed: Proven, Practical Ways to Raise Good Kids by Peter L. Benson, Judy Galbraith, and Pamela Espeland (Minneapolis: Free Spirit Publishing, 1994). Over 900 suggestions to help adults build Developmental Assets in children at home, at school, and in the community.

ORGANIZATIONS/WEB SITES

Character Education Partnership (CEP)
1025 Connecticut Avenue NW, Suite 1011
Washington, DC 20036
800-988-8081
www.character.com
A nonprofit organization dedicated to promoting character education at all grade levels. The Web site contains downloadable publications, lesson plans, a character education blog, and a substantive list of resources.

Collaborative for Academic, Social, and Emotional Learning (CASEL)
University of Illinois at Chicago
Department of Psychology
1007 W. Harrison Street
Chicago, IL 60607
312-413-1008
www.casel.org
An organization dedicated to promoting and advancing the practice of SEL. The Web site offers information and resources on all aspects of SEL advocacy and implementation.

The Center for Social Emotional Education (CSEE)
1841 Broadway, Suite 1212
New York, NY 10023
800-998-4701
www.csee.net
An organization that helps schools integrate crucial social and emotional learning with academic instruction.

Educators for Social Responsibility
23 Garden Street
Cambridge, MA 02138
800-370-2515
www.esrnational.org
A national nonprofit organization that works with educators to advocate practices such as SEL, character development, conflict resolution, diversity education, civic engagement, and more. The Web site contains lesson plans, activities, articles, and links for teachers of all grades.

GoodCharacter.com

www.goodcharacter.com

Recommended by the Parents' Choice Foundation, this Web site contains resources for character development and service learning. Includes articles, tips, teaching guides, lesson plans, and resource lists.

Learning Peace

www.learningpeace.com

This site helps educators, parents, and other adults create more peace in schools, homes, and communities by teaching children conflict resolution, anger management, anti-bullying, and character building.

Search Institute

The Banks Building
615 First Avenue NE, Suite 125
Minneapolis, MN 55413
800-888-7828
www.search-institute.org

Through dynamic research and analysis, this independent nonprofit organization works to promote healthy, active, and content youth and communities through asset building.

Teaching Tolerance

The Southern Poverty Law Center
400 Washington Avenue
Montgomery, AL 36104
334-956-8200
www.tolerance.org

A national education project dedicated to helping teachers foster respect and understanding in the classroom. The Web site contains resources for educators, parents, teens, and kids.

WestEd

730 Harrison Street
San Francisco, CA 94107
877-493-7833
www.wested.org

A research, development, and service agency that enhances and increases education and human development within schools, families, and communities.

ABOUT THE AUTHOR

Katia S. Petersen, Ph.D., is an author, consultant, and educator. She is a training expert in school climate improvement, student support, teacher coaching, and parent engagement. She has delivered professional development courses in schools nationwide on how to use literature to infuse social and emotional learning into core academics. Katia has trained over 65,000 educators and parents to enhance school success.

Katia has received many accolades and awards for her work with children and schools. They include having her books named in the "Top Ten Books" by the National Association of Elementary School Principals; being honored with a Teacher's Choice: Excellence in the Classroom Award from *Teacher Magazine*; and winning the National Association of Broadcasters Service to Children's Television Award.

Katia is the creator of the Safe & Caring Schools program for grades preK–8. She is the president and founder of Petersen Argo, Inc., a consulting firm that has been serving the educational needs of children and adults since 1990. She lives with her family in San Francisco, California.

For more information about Katia, the Safe & Caring Schools program, and training opportunities, check out www.safeandcaringschools.com.

The Safe & Caring Schools® Series

by Katia S. Petersen, Ph.D.

FLEXIBLE RESOURCE GUIDES THAT BLEND LEARNING WITH LIFE SKILLS AND CHARACTER DEVELOPMENT

Practical activities, monthly themes, and a foundation of literature make it easy to integrate social and emotional learning into the school day. Teacher-created and kid-tested, each resource guide contains complete lesson plans, fun activities, a monthly list of themes with literature connections, reproducible activity sheets, tips for organizing a schoolwide program, and a CD-ROM of all the reproducible activity sheets.

EACH BOOK: *$39.95, Softcover, 208 pp., 8½" x 11", reproducibles, with CD-ROM (Macintosh and Windows compatible)*

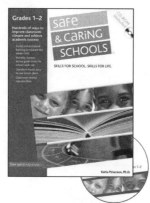

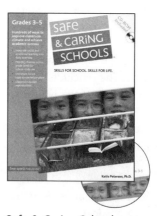

Safe & Caring Schools
PreK–K
BOOK WITH CD-ROM

Safe & Caring Schools
Grades 1–2
BOOK WITH CD-ROM

Safe & Caring Schools
Grades 3–5
BOOK WITH CD-ROM

Safe & Caring Schools
Grades 6–8
BOOK WITH CD-ROM

Key features of the Safe & Caring Schools Resources:

MONTHLY THEMES COORDINATED ACROSS ALL GRADE LEVELS

- My Safe & Caring School and Me
- Discovering Our Feelings
- My Support System
- Respect Yourself and Others
- Bullying Prevention
- Teaming Up for Success
- Conflict Resolution
- The Power to Choose
- Follow Your Dreams

SKILLS FOR SCHOOL. SKILLS FOR LIFE.

- Positive behaviors and attitudes
- Prevention of problem behaviors
- Empowering children to be part of the solution
- Getting along with others and celebrating diversity
- Believing in yourself
- Respect and care for others
- Positive adult role models for children
- Thriving as individuals and as part of groups

RESEARCH FOUNDATION

- Tested in various school models and with students of all abilities and backgrounds
- Scientifically-based research shows that social and emotional learning significantly improves students' academic performance
- Teaching approach that educates the whole child
- Integrates social and emotional learning into academic lessons

IMPLEMENTATION PLAN

- Works in all schools
- Use schoolwide or in single classrooms
- Sequential, yet flexible, activities
- Literature-based
- Year-long options
- Activities integrated with core curriculum
- Reproducible activity sheets, also on CD-ROM
- Safe & Caring vocabulary
- Use in morning meetings, advisory time, and throughout the day
- Staff training available

The Safe & Caring Schools® Posters

Ten posters reinforce the lessons and key skills from the Safe & Caring Schools resource guides. Use in classrooms, hallways, and gathering areas throughout the school. All posters are laminated and can be purchased individually or as a set.

EACH POSTER: *$8.95, Laminated, 18" x 24"*
SET OF 10 POSTERS: *$79.95*

POSTERS INCLUDE:
- Ambassadors of Peace
- Break the Silence
- Cool Enough to Care
- Golden Rule
- Be a Good Listener
- Safe & Caring Rules
- Stand Up for What You Believe In
- Stop, Think, Choose
- We Are a Safe & Caring School
- When I Get Angry

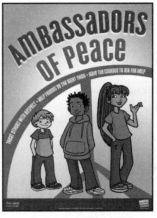
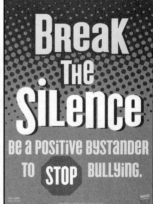

To place an order or to request a free catalog of Self-Help for Kids® and Self-Help for Teens® materials, please write, call, email, or visit our Web site:

Free Spirit Publishing Inc.
217 Fifth Avenue North • Suite 200 • Minneapolis, MN 55401-1299
toll-free 800.735.7323 • local 612.338.2068 • fax 612.337.5050
help4kids@freespirit.com • www.freespirit.com

More great books from free spirit

The Kid's Guide to Service Projects
Over 500 Service Ideas for Young People Who Want to Make a Difference
by Barbara A. Lewis

Hundreds of ideas for service projects, from simple to large-scale community efforts. Endorsed by Youth Service America. For ages 10 & up. $12.95; 184 pp.; softcover; 6" x 9"

What Do You Stand For? For Kids
A Guide to Building Character
by Barbara A. Lewis

True stories, inspiring quotations, thought-provoking dilemmas, and activities help elementary school children build positive character traits including caring, fairness, respect, and responsibility. From the best-selling author of What Do You Stand For? For Teens. For ages 7–12. $14.95; 176 pp.; softcover; B&W photos and illust.; 7¼" x 9"

What Do You Stand For? 96 Character Stickers
$5.95; Set of 96 stickers on 6 sheets (each sticker about 1" x 1¾")

The Complete Guide to Service Learning
Proven, Practical Ways to Engage Students in Civic Responsibility, Academic Curriculum, & Social Action
by Cathryn Berger Kaye, M.A.

A treasury of activities, ideas, quotes, reflections, resources, hundreds of annotated "Bookshelf" recommendations, and author interviews, presented within a curricular context and organized by theme. This eloquent, exhilarating guide can help teachers and youth workers engage young hearts and minds in reaching out and giving back. For teachers, grades K–12. $29.95; 240 pp.; softcover; illust.; 8½" x 11"

Ready to Rock Kids, Volume 1
CD and Activity Book
by Dr. Mac & Friends

Twelve original songs and more than 60 activities teach and reinforce positive thinking, respect, responsibility, including everyone, good manners, friendship, self-esteem, best effort, honesty, kindness, and more. For ages 4–9.

Ready to Rock Kids, Volume 2
CD and Activity Book
by Dr. Mac & Friends

Twelve original songs and more than 60 activities teach and reinforce caring, sharing, resilience, the Golden Rule, valuing diversity, learning and asking questions, taking care of things, peacemaking, and more. For ages 4–9.
Each Book: $16.95; 48 pp.; softcover; illust.; 8½" x 11"

I Can Play It Safe
by Alison Feigh, illustrated by Laura Logan

Written by an expert in child safety, this full-color picture book includes the check-in rule, safe versus harmful touch, and having trusted adults to turn to for help. This book helps children make smart choices about their personal safety every day. For ages 4–8, parents, teachers, counselors. $14.95; 32 pp.; hardcover; color illust.; 10" x 7½"

On Those Runaway Days
by Alison Feigh, illustrated by Laura Logan

When children feel overwhelmed, angry, or unsafe at home or in school, they may see running away as a solution to their worries. This book provides kids with an important set of coping strategies to use on those "runaway days." For ages 6–10, parents, teachers, counselors. $14.95; 32 pp.; hardcover; color illust.; 10" x 7½"

Bullies Are a Pain in the Brain
written and illustrated by Trevor Romain

Practical suggestions and humor help kids become "Bully-Proof," stop bullies from hurting others, and know what to do in dangerous situations. For ages 8–13. $8.95; 112 pp.; softcover, illust.; 5⅛" x 7"

Growing Good Kids
28 Activities to Enhance Self-Awareness, Compassion, and Leadership
by Deb Delisle and Jim Delisle, Ph.D.

Created by teachers and classroom-tested, these fun and meaningful enrichment activities build children's skills in problem solving, decision making, cooperative learning, divergent thinking, and communication. For grades 3–8. $29.95; 168 pp.; softcover; illust.; 8½" x 11"

Bully Free® Bulletin Boards, Posters, and Banners
Creative Displays for a Safe and Caring School, Grades K–8
by Allan L. Beane, Ph.D., and Linda Beane

Support and reinforce an anti-bullying program or spread the word that bullying won't be tolerated. This book describes 50 displays (25 for elementary school, 25 for middle school) that kids can create for classrooms, hallways, and other school areas, with instruction and reinforcement from teachers. Each project includes instructions, art templates, visuals, and discussion questions. For grades K–8. $24.95; 144 pp.; softcover; illust., 8½" x 11", lay-flat binding

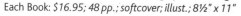

www.freespirit.com